The Monument
Art and Vulgarity in Saddam Hussein's Iraq

Kanan Makiya

Essential reading for anyone concerned about the relationship between art and politics, particularly in Iraq

". . . brilliant and moving . . ."—*New York Review of Books*

"Makiya writes stridently . . . he is capable of patient rational analysis unraveling what the Monument teaches about the abuse of art for political purposes."—*Times Literary Supplement*

IN BAGHDAD, AN ENORMOUS MONUMENT NEARLY TWICE THE SIZE OF THE ARC de Triomphe towers over the city. Two huge forearms emerge from the ground, clutching two swords that clash overhead. Those arms are enlarged casts of those of Saddam Hussein, showing every bump and follicle. The "Victory Arch" celebrates a victory over Iran (in their eight-year long war) that never happened. *The Monument* is a study of the interplay between art and politics, of how culture, normally an unquestioned good, can play into the hands of power with devastating effects. Kanan Makiya uses the culture invented by Saddam Hussein as a window into the nature of totalitarianism and shows how art can become the weapon of dictatorship.

KANAN MAKIYA directs the Iraq Research Project at Harvard University, and is a professor at Brandies University. He was also involved with the US's planning of the war in Iraq.

1-86064-966-1 ◎ 167 pp. ◎ Price $18.95

The MONUMENT

By the same author

Republic of Fear

The MONUMENT

Kanan Makiya

I.B. Tauris

New edition published in 2004 by I.B. Tauris & Co. Ltd
6 Salem Road, London W2 4BU
175 Fifth Avenue, New York, NY 10010
www.ibtauris.com

In the United States of America and in Canada distributed by
Palgrave Macmillan, a division of St Martins Press, 175 Fifth
Avenue, New York NY 10010

First published in 1991 by the University of California Press
Copyright © Kanan Makiya, 1991, 2004

ISBN 1 86064 966 1

A full CIP record for this book is available from the British Library
A full CIP record for this book is available from the Library of Congress

Library of Congress catalog card: available

Printed and bound in Great Britain by MPG Books Ltd, Bodmin.

To my mother

Illustrations

13. Looking towards Haifa street across the old city. Photo: Steve McCurry/ Magnum.

14. 'Post-Modern' buildings of the 1980s in Baghdad. Photo: Steve McCurry/ Magnum.

15. The *Shaheed* (Martyrs') Monument, Baghdad. Ismail Fattah, 1983. Photo: Steve McCurry/Magnum.

16. Artist's impression of *Shaheed* Monument. Reproduced from the pamphlet *Nasb Shuhadaa' Qadisiyyat Saddam*, Amanat al-Assima, Baghdad, 1983.

17. The Unknown Soldier Monument, Baghdad. Khalid al-Rahal, 1982. Reproduced courtesy of *Process: Architecture*, issue no. 58, May 1985.

18. The Unknown Soldier Monument. Close-up view of tilted shield.

19. Sculpture park. Basra, 1989. Photo: Tom Stoddart/Katz.

20. Triumphal Arch. Adolf Hitler, 1925. Reproduced courtesy of Bundesarchiv.

21. Campbell's Soup Can. Andy Warhol, 1964. Silkscreen on canvas, 35¾ × 24 ins. Copyright 1990 The Estate and Foundation of Andy Warhol.

22. Gold wristwatch. Photo: Steve McCurry/Magnum.

23. Inside a café. Photo: Steve McCurry/Magnum.

24. Peasant dwelling in southern Iraq. Photo: Homer Sykes/Network.

25. Desert billboard. Photo: Homer Sykes/Woodfin Camp.

26. The Monument viewed along the ceremonial axis and showing both arches. Saddam Husain, 1989. Photo: private collection.

27. Viewing stand, ceremonial axis, fireworks and Victory Arch in the far distance. Photo: Versele–Photo News/Spooner.

28. Bab al-Nasr (the gate of victory) in Cairo. Reproduced from *Description de l'Egypte*, 23 vols., Paris, Imprimerie impériale, 1809–28.

29. Billboard of Saddam Husain astride the Ishtar Gate. Photo: Stuart Franklin/ Magnum.

30. The Monument. Detail of helmets and base. Saddam Husain, Baghdad, 1989.

31. The Monument. Detail of flag and crossed swords. Saddam Husain, Baghdad, 1989.

32. A hot-dog stand in Los Angeles. Courtesy of Charles Jencks, *The Language of Post-Modern Architecture* (London: Academy Editions, 1979).

33. Robert Venturi's recommendation for a monument. Courtesy of Venturi, Scott Brown and Associates, Inc.

34. Baghdad State Mosque Competition, Minoru Takeyama, 1983. Reproduced from *State Mosque Competition: Baghdad, Iraq*, a publication of Amanat al-Asima (project no. 651/328), Baghdad, 1983.

35. Baghdad State Mosque Competition, Venturi, Rauch and Scott Brown, 1983. Reproduced from *State Mosque Competition: Baghdad, Iraq*, a publication of Amanat al-Asima (project no. 651/328), Baghdad, 1983.

36. Section through dome, Baghdad State Mosque Competition, Venturi, Rauch and Scott Brown, 1983. Reproduced from *State Mosque Competition: Baghdad, Iraq*, a publication of Amanat al-Asima (project no. 651/328), Baghdad, 1983.

37. Interior view of main prayer hall, Baghdad State Mosque Competition, Venturi, Rauch and Scott Brown, 1983. Reproduced from *State Mosque Competition: Baghdad, Iraq*, a publication of Amanat al-Asima (project no. 651/328), Baghdad, 1983.

38. 'Clothespin'. Claes Oldenburg, 1976. Height: 13.5 metres, Philadelphia. Photo: Leo Castelli Gallery.

39. The Ishtar Gate at half-size. Photo: Stuart Franklin/Magnum.

40. A guard at the palace of Nebuchadnezzar. Photo: Tom Stoddart/Woodfin Camp.

41. 'Shahrazad and Shahryar'. Mohammed Ghani, 1975. Bronze, 4.25 metres, Abu Nuwas street, Baghdad.

42. The Fountain of Kuhrumaneh. Mohammed Ghani, 1971. Bronze, 3.30 metres, Sa'adoon street, Baghdad.

43. Iraqi flag/sculpture in *Shaheed* Monument. Metal, 5.0 metres high, Baghdad.

44. Babylon Hotel, Baghdad.

45. Ministry of Industry Building, Baghdad.

46. Richmond Riverside Development, London. Quinlan Terry, 1988. Courtesy of Erith and Terry Architects.

47. Minaret detail from Suleyman Mosque, Jedda. Abdel Wahed al-Wakil, 1980. Reproduced from *Albenaa*, no. 34, vol. 6, April–May 1987.

48. *Nasb al-Hurriyya* (the Freedom Monument). Bronze castings on travertine clad slab, 50 metres × 10 metres. Jewad Salim, 1961. Reproduced courtesy of *Process: Architecture*, issue no. 58, May 1985.

49. *Nasb al-Hurriyya*. Detail of horse.

50. *Nasb al-Hurriyya*. The first half in detail.

51. *Nasb al-Hurriyya*. Detail of 'martyrdom' and 'motherhood' castings.

52. *Nasb al-Hurriyya*. Detail of political prisoner being released.

53. 'Man and the Earth'. Jewad Salim, 1955. Plaster relief, 45cm × 45cm.

54. 'Children Playing'. Jewad Salim, 1953–54. Oil on canvas.

55. 'The Unknown Political Prisoner'. Jewad Salim, 1952. Plaster maquette for international competition submission.

56. Carved wooden door. Mohammed Ghani, 1964.

57. 'A Horseman'. Faiq Hasan, 1980s. Oil on canvas.

58. 'The Struggling Leader Saddam Husain with the People'. Mahood Ahmad, 1980s. Oil on canvas.

59. The old Unknown Soldier Monument in Sa'adoun square, Baghdad. Rifa'at Chadirchi, early 1960s. Reproduced courtesy of *Process: Architecture*, issue no. 58, May 1985.

60. Ctesiphon arch just south of Baghdad. Built in the third century AD. Reproduced from Richard Coke, *The Heart of the Middle East* (London: Thornton Butterworth, 1925).

61. The Khulafa Mosque. Mohammed Makiya, 1963. Old and new brick details.

Acknowledgements

Friends originating in five countries thousands of miles apart, have read and commented upon this manuscript. I owe them more than a scholarly debt of acknowledgement. For they are the reference points which I lean upon to take a stand in this world. The day is coming when it will be possible to name them on a page like this. That day is not here yet.

My editor, Esther Whitby, believed in this book long before it became all too easy to do so. My reader, Robert Harbison, asked some very difficult questions. These helped clarify underlying intentions to the great benefit of the final work. No one has ever read something I wrote with such care and intelligence. My publisher, Tom Rosenthal, took a risk when so many others before him would not. People like this are what publishing a book is supposed to be all about.

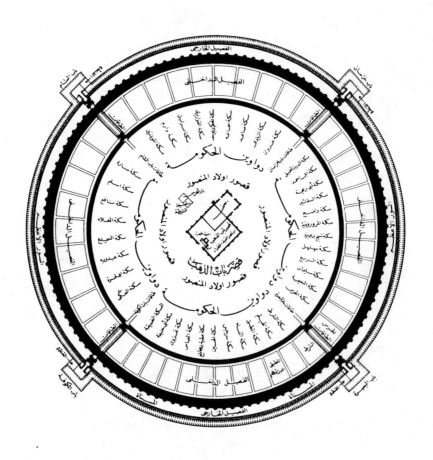

The Round City of al-Mansur[1]

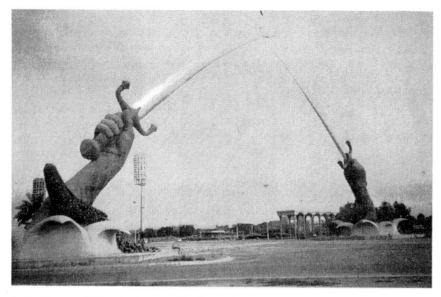

1. The Monument. Otherwise known as 'The Victory Arch', Baghdad, 1989.

Preamble

On 8 August 1989, an important new monument was opened to the Iraqi public. The invitation card sent to selected guests rightly describes it as 'one of the largest works of art in the world' (Fig. 1 and 2). The 'Victory Arch', as it is called, was conceived by the President of Iraq, Saddam Husain, who first announced the plan in a speech on 22 April 1985. His initial sketch and an extract from that speech were reproduced on the invitation card (Fig. 3). The final scheme was worked out with the help of an eminent Iraqi sculptor, Khalid al-Rahal, and executed under the President's close supervision. When Rahal died early on in the project, his role passed to another eminent Iraqi sculptor, Mohammed Ghani.

1

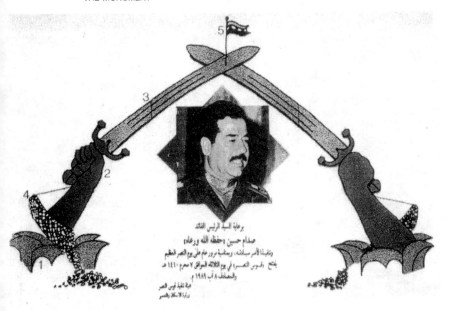

2. The Monument as depicted on the invitation card sent to selected guests on opening day and issued by the 'Executive Committee for the Victory Arch', from the Ministry of Housing and Construction. The Arabic text reads:

'Under the guidance of the Leader-President, Saddam Husain (God preserve and watch over him), and in execution of the orders of His Excellency, and on the occasion of one year passing since the day of the great victory, the "Victory Arch" will be opened on Tuesday Muharram 7, 1410 [Muslim calendar] which coincides with August 8, 1989 AD.'

On the back of the card the 'design idea' is spelled out:

'The ground bursts open and from it springs the arm that represents power and determination, carrying the sword of Qadisiyya. It is the arm of the Leader-President, Saddam Husain himself (God preserve and watch over him) enlarged forty times. It springs out to announce the good news of victory to all Iraqis, and it pulls in its wake a net that has been filled with the helmets of the enemy soldiers, some of them scattering into the wasteland.'

The 'elements' of the Victory Arch are broken down as follows (I have added identifying numbers to the drawing to correspond to the breakdown):

'(1) The Exploding Ground: made from reinforced concrete with enemy helmets scattered above; (2) The Forearm and the Grip: cast in bronze and weighing 20 tons each, fixed on to a steel frame also weighing 20 tons; (3) The Sword: the sword of Qadisiyya was used with a slight bend in order to give the arched shape. It is made of stainless steel. Each sword weighs 24 tons. The grip and the martyrs' dome [?] were cast in bronze and weigh 4 tons each; (4) The Net: cast in bronze, each net contains 2,500 helmets taken from the Iranian enemy; (5) The Flag: made from stainless steel and rising 7 metres above the meeting point of the two swords. The stainless steel used in the project (the swords) was made from the weapons of the martyrs and weighs 42.6 tons.'

2

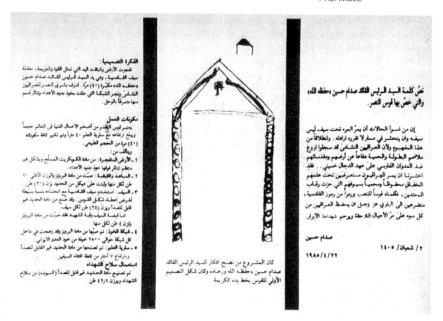

3. Back view of the invitation card showing 'the preliminary sketch for the arch by his venerable hand' in the centre. On the left are the 'idea' and 'elements' of the design translated in Fig. 2. On the right is the extract from Husain's speech of 22 April 1985, which reads:

'The worst condition is for a person to pass under a sword which is not his own or to be forced down a road which is not willed by him. From this, and because brave Iraqis have recorded the most legendary exploits in defence of their land and holy beliefs against the Persian enemy in the era of the liar Khomeini . . . we have chosen that Iraqis will pass under their fluttering flag protected by their swords which have cut through the necks of the aggressors. And so we have willed it an arch to victory, and a symbol to this Qadisiyya . . .'

The maquette was worked from plaster casts of the President's arms, taken from just above the elbow, with a sword inserted into each fist. The monument serves as a Ba'thi equivalent of the Arc de Triomphe in the Champs Elysées. The Ba'thi arch, however, is bigger. The President's forearms and fists, sixteen metres in length (the same height as the Arc de Triomphe), burst out of the ground like gargantuan bronze tree-trunks and rise with their firmly grasped swords to an apex forty metres above the ground. War debris in the shape of five thousand Iranian helmets taken fresh from the battelfield are gathered up in two nets (2,500 in each) which are torn asunder at

3

the base, scattering the helmets around the points at which the arms rise from the earth.

Because no Iraqi foundry was big enough, the arms were cast in sections at the Morris Singer foundry in Basingstoke, England — the largest professional art foundry in the world. The swords, on the other hand, were cast in Iraq, and the official invitation card informs us that the raw steel used was obtained by melting down the weapons of Iraqi 'martyrs' who died in the fighting.

Saddam Husain's monument has been built in duplicate, marking the two entrances of a vast new parade-ground in central Baghdad (see Fig. 26). The pair of arches were opened to the public by the President, who was televised riding under them along a connecting ceremonial axis on a white stallion.

This essay is an attempt to think through the meaning of this offering to the city.

Art is always realistic, because it tries to create for men that
which is foremost their reality. Art is always idealistic,
because all reality that art creates is a product of the mind.

Conrad Fiedler[2]

1
The Art
of the Monument

Consider the monument as an object in its own right. In particular,
consider the aesthetic significance of the casting technique employed in
its making. Why not model or carve the President's limbs before
setting them for all time in bronze? In the fashion of ancient Greek
sculpture, why wasn't the executing artist encouraged to imagine them
even more perfectly than they really were, or ever could be? One
could then have avoided the numerous little hair follicles, the odd
scratch and blemish. Why do the lines and curvature of the muscles
and protruding veins have to register as an exact replica of those on the
President's body, at this particular age, on that particular day? Could

any viewer tell the difference, driving past in a car, or even walking down the street at close quarters?

Maybe Saddam Husain's monument is unworthy of serious discussion. Accident, a passing fancy, or even the whispered suggestion of a sycophant, might account for the decision to have the President's own arms serve as the model. In any case hardly anyone today thinks of art as perfect imitation, notwithstanding Plato and Aristotle. Art, we are now accustomed to think, is about self-expression, form-making, the creation out of nothing and for nothing; not about copying the literal reality. If art is imitation, Conrad Fiedler argues, then the artist is 'encroaching upon nature's creative work – a childish, senseless enterprise, which often takes on the appearance of a certain ingenious boldness, usually based on absence of thought'.[3] The art of Saddam Husain, it would seem, is thus disqualified from discussion by virtue of the very casting technique which he himself in all probability insisted on.[4]

However, insofar as there is some genuine artistic impulse present in this object, it exists precisely in the apparently irrelevant technical choice of making a plaster cast of the arms of Saddam Husain, deliberately eschewing all other alternatives. Moral considerations aside, a perceptible moment of artistic cognition is embedded in this choice, even though by itself this moment is not sufficient to render the object as a whole a 'work of art', whatever that might be taken to mean. (A visual impulse or insight of an artistic nature is not, after all, uncommon in the ordinary person, although we frequently convince ourselves otherwise. The best evidence for this lies in the promise shown by children's drawings, which gets overlaid in later years by the emphasis on verbal and numerate skills.)

The choice of casting – rather than modelling or carving or assembling – produces a perfect fit between intention, built form and the inner experience of the outside world in Ba'thi Iraq (Fig. 4). The knowledge that in every little bump and squiggle which can be seen, felt and maybe even stroked, these were, are and will always remain His arms is mesmerizing. The effect must not rest on a lie any more than the divine image on the Turin Shroud can afford to be shown by carbon-dating tests to be a fourteenth-century fake. Only casting renders absolute authority (which is singular and abstract, yet experienced in all the minutiae of daily life in Iraq) visible and

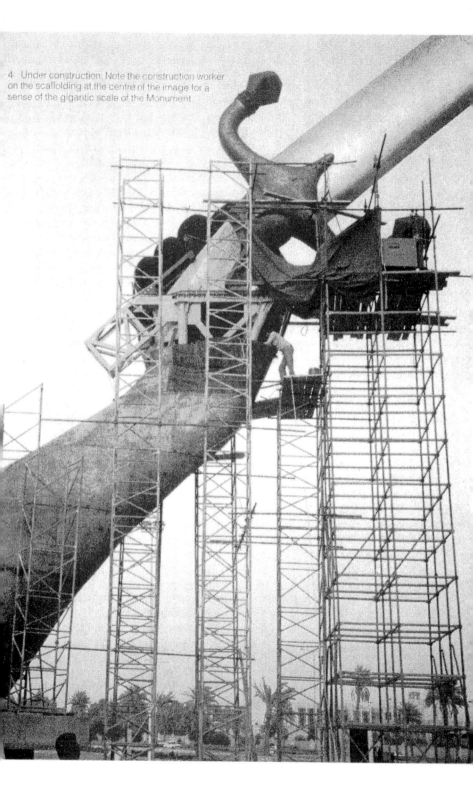

4 Under construction. Note the construction worker on the scaffolding at the centre of the image for a sense of the gigantic scale of the Monument.

corporeal while retaining the aura of absolute uniqueness, so essential to a work of art even in this age of mechanical reproduction.[5] (I am assuming of course that the original maquette would be destroyed and copies in the future would have to be made by modelling from the monument at full scale.)

The same literal intelligence present in the use of the President's forearms is evident in two other elements of the scheme: the use of the five thousand Iranian war helmets, and of the weapons of Iraqi soldiers melted down to make the raw steel of the sword blades. To look at the helmets in the knowledge that their scratches, dents and bullet holes were made by real bullets, that actual skulls might have exploded inside, is just as awe-inspiring as the knowledge that these are not anybody's arms, but the President's own. Or, for that matter, that not any old steel was used in the sword blades, but only that taken from Iraqi 'martyrs'.

If the idea of melting down broken machine guns and tanks in order to fabricate the swords sounds far-fetched, this was nonetheless the contention of Iraqi officialdom (who is to say or know otherwise?), and is supported by circumstantial evidence. The British foundry, Morris Singer, only cast the bronze items (principally the forearms); these were then transported in sections to Iraq by lorry convoy (in exactly the same manner as the 'superguns', parts of which were confiscated by British and Greek customs in April—May 1990). The sword blades, forty metres or so in length, were fabricated in a local Iraqi foundry specially adapted for the purpose, with the assistance of foreign expertise. Why go to such extraordinary lengths for a one-off commission if it were not all-important to carry the underlying ideology through into physical reality?

The activity of art, however literally or abstractly imagined, is founded in a perceptual mastering of the visible or felt world by some still mysterious power of the human mind. An artistic moment of cognition seems to happen when this power, driven by inner necessity not outer compulsion, seeks to grapple with the disaggregated jumble of sensual reality, the world of appearances and feelings, imparting to it a newly created yet decipherable form. Such a moment came to the maker of this monument.

Many more people can experience a work of art than can make one. The experience of art, as distinct from its activity, happens when the object succeeds in triggering back into human consciousness that same sensual reality which had previously energized the artist, however unconsciously. The evocative power of this monument lies in the fact that by employing the technique of casting, by using real Iranian helmets and melting down the weapons of dead Iraqi soldiers, Saddam Husain the artist froze into form a fundamental truth about Saddam Husain the Leader.

Mass propaganda discovered that its audience was ready at all
times to believe the worst, no matter how absurd, and did not
particularly object to being deceived because it held every
statement to be a lie anyhow ... Leaders based their
propaganda on the correct psychological assumption that,
under such conditions, one could make people believe the
most fantastic statements one day, and trust that if the next
day they were given irrefutable proof of their falsehood, they
would take refuge in cynicism; instead of deserting the leaders
who had lied to them, they would protest that they had
known all along that the statement was a lie and would
admire the leaders for their superior tactical cleverness.

Hannah Arendt[6]

2
The Symbolism
of the Monument

The monument was erected shortly after what the regime deems to
have been a 'victory' in the Iraq–Iran war, and it was erected to
commemorate that victory. Yet it was commissioned several hundred
thousand lives earlier, in 1985, when no victory was in sight. Its
conception therefore precedes the reality it is meant to commemorate,
which is most uncommon in the history of monument making.

The swords that Saddam Husain is holding up are meant to
represent the defeat of the Persian Sassanian empire by the invading
Arab-Muslim army in the battle of Qadisiyya in AD 637, a defeat
which paved the way for the Islamicization of Iran. The Iraq–Iran war
from the start was always referred to by Ba'thi propaganda as

Qadisiyyat Saddam, meaning the Iraqi President's new (or own) Qadisiyya. The holy (for Arabs) and aggressive (for Iranians) implication of calling it such was not lost on the region. The swords are those of Sa'ad ibn-abi-Waqas, the commander of the Muslim army that defeated the Persians and an honoured companion of the prophet Muhammad himself. By analogy, therefore, Saddam Husain is at the very least the Sa'ad ibn-abi-Waqas of the 1980s (Fig. 5).

This is how the symbolism is intended to work. The problem is that no one really knows what Sa'ad ibn-abi-Waqas's sword looked like. Probably it looked like any other sword (Fig. 6). We have to be told what it is. In the original maquette, the two swords were not identical. One was the sword of Qadisiyya, whilst the other was *dhu 'l Faqar*, the sword with magical attributes which first belonged to the prophet Muhammad and was obtained by him as booty in the battle of Badr. This sword does have an instantly recognizable physical form. In Muslim iconography *dhu 'l Faqar* is represented with two points, used to put out both eyes of the enemy in a single thrust. Most importantly, however, the sword was passed on to 'Ali-ibn-abi-Talib, the cousin of the Prophet and patron saint of Shi'ism. Eventually it became identified with him, surviving the centuries as a key symbol of Shi'ism.

Was this sword eliminated in the built version of the monument for aesthetic reasons (perhaps it spoiled the symmetry of the arch, especially at the apex where the swords cross)? I don't know. From the point of view of the regime's own symbolism, however, it ought to have been retained. To depict the Sunni leader Saddam Husain killing Iranians with the sword of 'Ali would be in the same spirit as having him inaugurate the monument by riding under it on a white stallion. The horse is a key symbol of Arab male pride, and whiteness signifies purity. But, more importantly, as every Shi'ite knows, when Husain the son of 'Ali was martyred on the plains of Kerbala in AD 680, he was riding a white horse. This is a very popular symbol. The annual Shi'i Muslim passion play performed in holy cities like Najaf and Kerbala, in southern Iraq, always shows Husain the son of 'Ali on a white horse (Figs. 7, 8, 9).

Is Saddam Husain, therefore, making the point that the 'Persian enemy' was beaten by Iraqi Arabs, Sunni and Shi'i alike? National unity prevailed in the face of foreign aggression; this is the Ba'thist line on the war. On the face of things it corresponds to an important truth;

11

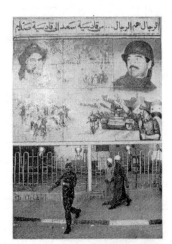

5. The top band of writing on this wallposter reads: 'The men who are [real] men ... From Qadisiyyat Sa'ad to Qadisiyyat Saddam.' Of course no one knows what Sa'ad ibn-abi-Waqas (top left) looked like.

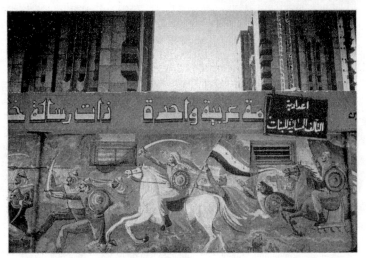

6. I assume the man riding the horse is Waqas. The writing at the top reads: 'One Arab nation with an eternal message.' Notice the modern Iraqi flag. The black title block of the writing is the name of an evening school for girls. Beyond the poster we can see the same buildings depicted in Fig. 14. Just as the flag represents a touch of modernity in a traditional scene, the windows of the buildings in the background introduce a touch of tradition into the worst kind of modern environment. The same mindset is at work, even though done by totally unrelated people (a professional architect and a popular illustrator).

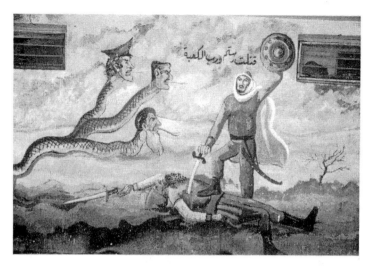

7. An Iraqi wallposter depicting a victorious Arab warrior with the severed head of an Iranian opponent. The most interesting stylistic feature is the extent to which it simulates popular Shi'ite imagery, especially as this was adapted in Iran after the revolution. The serpent-like figures are Khomeini, Hafaz Asad and Ghaddafi. The Arabic lettering reads: 'By the Lord of the Ka'aba, I have killed Rustam.' Rustam is the great pre-Islamic Persian hero (like Achilles to the Greeks).

an army of Shi'i soldiers and Sunni officers in a deeply divided society did not fracture along sectarian lines as the clerical leadership in Tehran had hoped it would throughout all the gruelling years of the war.

The key to this revamped Arab-Muslim historical symbolism is to be found in a 1979 speech in which Saddam Husain claimed to be a 'descendant of 'Ali'. It occurs again in his semi-official biography which published a family tree providing 'proof' of this claim (Fig. 10).[7] Does factual uncertainty surround the Sunniism of Saddam Husain? Hardly. Born and brought up in the Sunni town of Takrit, in a traditional quarter populated with the very same relatives upon whom he largely relies in government today, the Sunniism of his origins is as absolute a fact as could ever exist in Iraq. So what is the point of making such a flagrant assertion?

However modern many Iraqis may have become by the 1980s, ordinary people still placed enormous value on the origins of men,

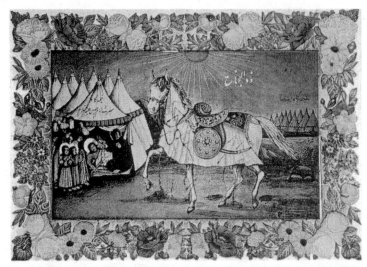

8. A popular Shi'i poster depicting the white horse of Husain the son of 'Ali, *dhu al-Jinah*, dripping blood and pierced with arrows, just after his master's martyrdom on the plains of Kerbala.

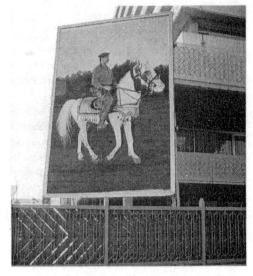

9. Portrait of Saddam Husain riding a white horse, as on 8 August 1989, at the opening of the Monument.

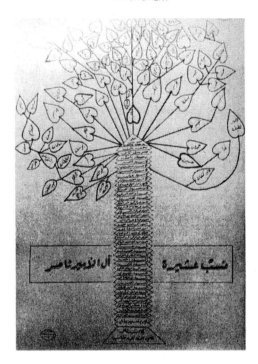

10. Saddam Husain's Family Tree. Saddam Husain's name appears in the large heart-shaped leaf on the far left of the crown of the tree. It is traced to an Ottoman ancestor named 'Umar Bek al-Thani (the third name down from the top of the trunk). The last name at the base of the tree is that of 'Ali ibn abi Talib, the fourth Muslim caliph and patron saint of Shi'ism. It would appear that the trunk of the tree represents the Muslim centuries ending with the fall of the Ottoman empire in 1918; the crown represents modern twentieth-century Iraq.

their family backgrounds, and primary confessional allegiances. The President is very conscious of these double-edged social facts, and sets out to wield them to political advantage. For instance, beneath a monument commemorating the Unknown Soldier which was erected in 1983 (see Fig. 18), the life story of Saddam Husain from birth through his early years as a militant, is presented to the public. Here, the concrete foundations for the monument double as an underground museum in which the story of the President is told by analogy with that of the Prophet (both having been brought up as orphans, by uncles, becoming militant activists and idealists, etc.).

Such repeated and well-calculated imagery has worked to solidify power in Iraq. Its success is built on something bigger than the President's personal proclivities and the persistence of traditional social realities; it attests to the power of mass propaganda when it corresponds to a deeply felt collective need to believe in a mythology such as victory in the Iraq−Iran war (or the omnipotence of a leader

15

who is at the foundation of a polity ostensibly based on tradition).

Such a deeply felt need arises only when the relationship between politics and society has gone profoundly awry through war, civil war or revolution, and tradition itself has completely lost its givenness. The need now is to create new traditions, new sources of coherence. By rising to selfconsciousness, the formerly unselfconscious changes. The unity of the community which can no longer be taken for granted is reduced to a frantic clinging to symbols and stock phrases, as though they were lifelines.

Thus the Islamic Shi'ite imagery of the Iranian revolution (the idea of the 'Great Satan', the uses of martyrdom, for instance) served the purpose of reconstituting a mythical Islam that had in fact never existed in quite this way before.[8] And even in completely fractured conditions of authority, the Lebanese warring sects assert a deep collective anxiety about their solidity as a community, by agreeing to identify the source of all evil in the machinations of outsiders – be they Israelis, Palestinians, Americans or Syrians. It is these outsiders who conspire to destroy an increasingly imaginary Lebanon that likewise never existed. In such troubled circumstances, the public becomes accustomed to clutching at any straw in its desire for some stable 'truth'. Belief in something easy and quick is required to reassure the community in its anxiety about itself. Without the lie of victory in the Iraq–Iran war, could the Iraqi polity have held together? This is a very real question. By the same token, however much the demons may change in the Lebanon, is there not a twisted hope for that country in the habit of always blaming others for the problems of Lebanese politics?

Every community is founded on uncritically held beliefs (the inviolability of the individual or the principle of tolerance are also beliefs which cannot be justified on purely rational grounds, any more than the divinity of Saddam Husain). Such prior beliefs, once become cultural norms, are as genuine as any later cynicism or incredulity at one's earlier beliefs. For the decision to believe 'can only be carried out successfully if accompanied by a decision to forget ... the decision to believe ... The loss of the critical faculty is not simply a by-product of the self-induced faith, but an essential condition for that faith to be held seriously.'[9] Unless new uncritically held beliefs replace the old, radical doubt sets in and collective decomposition ensues.

Hence, in difficult times, the urge to believe in almost anything.

Any sword would have done, but Saddam Husain holds up the swords of the holy wars of Islam to wage war not against infidels, but against an Islamic republic. And he drives through his arches not on a modern tank, but on a white horse even though he is intent on overthrowing a Shi'ite revolution. On another level, therefore, his monument, like his biography, is a bald political assertion in the teeth of known facts (like his Sunniism, his nationalism and the fact that the war's outcome was a standoff, not a victory). Granted that the people for a while will accept anything because they have a need to, is the President simply a liar?

To an inveterate political actor like Saddam Husain the contingency of any human fact is irksome. The quintessential professional militant, he rose from nothing as a teenager in the Iraqi branch of the Ba'th party. The boy had first made his mark in a minority party by assassinating a prominent supporter of the Iraqi President, 'Abdul Karim Qassem, in his home town of Takrit. Subsequently he was chosen to join a hit team that failed to kill Qassem in 1959. Then came years in the political wilderness, followed by power in 1968, and the ruthless elimination of opposition parties, Ba'thi rivals, colleagues, friends. Such a man had become habituated to making his own reality virtually from scratch. For someone with a taste for ideologizing the world, this meant that reality could be made to fit almost any set of facts. The President *feels* himself to be a master of the past through the spinning of theories and analogies in the same absolute way that he actually is master of the present. He does not think of himself as a liar, but as a theorist whose current reality is always 'proof' of any assertion he chooses to make.

But to an outsider the sword of Qadisiyya in the fist of Saddam Husain, towering over the debris of a nation believed to have been abjectly defeated, is stunning new proof of the same fantastic lie which Iraqis in pre-Ba'thi days would have known to be such although they had to pretend otherwise. Eventually many ended up genuinely believing the lie they had at first only pretended to believe. This is still a culture that places as much value on the representation of a thing as it does on the thing itself. And finally, like all cultures, it has to believe in something. Everything else has been taken away. Only the imagery of Saddam Husain's Qadisiyya is left.

The litmus test of absolute authority is this capability of turning lies into truth. Victory, Saddam's Qadisiyya, the President's Shi'ite lineage — these are the lie become truth inside Iraq because it passes uncontradicted. The Turin Shroud, after all, was not proved a forgery for seven hundred years. What happened, in the meantime, one wonders, to the cardinals, bishops and simple priests who, like Plato's philosopher-king in *The Republic*, conspired to found their legitimacy on such an ingenious lie, likewise intended to consolidate belief?[10]

Monuments are the expression of man's highest cultural
needs. They have to satisfy the eternal demand of the people
for translation of their collective force into symbols. The
most vital monuments are those which express the feeling and
thinking of this collective force — the people.
   Every bygone period which shaped a real cultural life had
the power and the capacity to create these symbols.
Monuments are, therefore, only possible in periods in which a
unifying consciousness and unifying culture exists. Periods
which exist for the moment have been unable to create lasting
monuments.

Jose Luis Sert (architect), Fernand Leger (painter) and Sigfried
   Giedion (theorist), 'Nine Points on Monumentality'[11]

3
The Monument
and the City

To understand the President's monument properly we must see it in a
wider context. For despite its idiosyncrasies it is not a total aberration
and is very much part of its city. For the construction of public
monuments in Baghdad has become something of a national obsession
in the last decade. Urban form has had to adapt itself around the larger
of the new edifices, and circulation patterns have changed. Streets and
squares are now marked by the presence of such artefacts, as they were
marked only a short time ago by the absence of the fabled city of the
Caliphs and One Thousand and One Nights.

   Baghdad never lived up to the romance of its name. Before Saddam
Husain's monument arrived, the streets were changing, growing wider

and ever more impersonal, crowding in the mosques and the courtyard houses of the old city quarters. In the 1950s and 1960s, the dirty, picturesque 'old' Baghdad – with its sectarian and ethnically divided neighbourhoods, its colourful souks, its horizontal skyline punctuated with pretty vertical minarets, its inward-looking houses and shaded narrow alleyways – was being destroyed, we are constantly reminded, by modern 'International Style' architecture and that rampant engine of individual freedom: the automobile (Figs. 11, 12). Today even that much maligned, anarchic and crumblingly cosmopolitan city of the 1960s has shed its skin. Under the same name, a new assertive metropolis of five million people has taken the place of the city which housed a mere quarter of a million people in the 1920s, and which had grown to one and a half million by 1968 when the Ba'th first came to power. Hence, a large and growing number of people who today live in the new monument-filled city of Baghdad, have in fact never lived in any other kind of city.

Baghdad first began to metamorphose into its present form in the late 1970s. The regime's efforts had previously been taken up with eliminating domestic opposition, a Kurdish civil war, infrastructure development, nationalizations, eradicating illiteracy, industrialization, and military buildup. After a decade in power focused on these issues, the Iraqi political leadership felt secure, united and self-assured: all necessary preconditions for the President's decision to go to war with Iran in the spring of 1980. Moreover, the nonaligned nations conference was scheduled to be held in Baghdad in the summer of 1982. Saddam Husain, who had just hosted the anti-Camp David Arab Summit, was going to take over the mantle of Third World leadership from Fidel Castro. And he was going to have this leadership bestowed upon him in his own city. The desire to construct monuments and to assert political authority coincided therefore, as they have done since time immemorial in virtually every civilization.

Overnight Baghdad became a giant construction site: new and wider roads, redevelopment zones, forty-five shopping centres in different parts of the city opened to the public by 1982, parks (including a new tourist centre on an artificial island in the Tigris), a plethora of new buildings designed by Iraqi and world class architects, a crash programme for a subway system, and many new monuments – all were put in hand. The time had come to crystallize political facts and

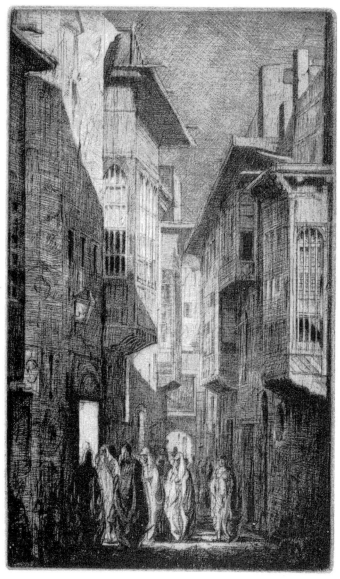

11. Engraving of typical alleyway in 'old' Baghdad, c.1920s (name of artist is illegible).

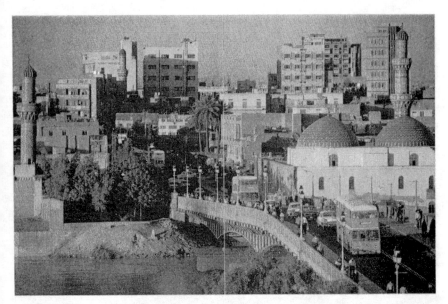

12. 1960s Baghdad: anarchic, schizoid, fragmented, but lively and human (photograph taken in early 1970s but no new buildings depicted and atmosphere still that of previous decade).

goals within the public realm in great architecture and lasting monumental art; to translate the collective force of the Iraqi people, as that leading theoretician of the modern movement Sigfried Giedion would have put it, into symbols.

The Mayor of Baghdad, Samir 'Abd al-Wahab al-Shaikhly, was fond of saying that twenty billion Iraqi dinars had been budgeted for this purpose. In particular six large areas in the central business and residential districts of Baghdad became in 1979 the focus of a massive accelerated urban redevelopment programme: Khulafa street, the Bab al-Sheikh area, the al-Kadhimmiyya shrine and vicinity, the al-Karkh area, Abu Nuwas street and Haifa street. The Khulafa street redevelopment, for instance, consists of many new buildings along the street, two squares, a civic centre, a huge mosque extension and the rehabilitation of some old quarters.

The outcome of at least some of that expenditure can be experienced in Haifa street which was opened amid much fanfare in 1985 (Figs. 13, 14). Nothing remotely like Haifa street has ever existed in Baghdad

22

before. And insofar as the environment in which people live has any influence on their behaviour, or sense of who they are as a community, it can safely be said that an Iraqi nurtured in the bosom of Haifa street will not resemble one nurtured in 'old' Baghdad, however one wished to define that long lost city.

Among the big monuments of the new city special note must be made of the highly acclaimed *Shaheed* Monument of 1983, consisting of a circular platform, 190 metres in diameter, floating over an underground museum and carrying a 40-metre high split dome. The ensemble sits in the middle of a huge artificial lake (Figs. 15, 16). It cost the Iraqi exchequer a quarter of a billion dollars. Built by the Mitsubishi Corporation to the very exacting specifications of the engineering consulting firm of Ove Arup and Partners (of Sydney Opera House fame), the monument was conceived by the gifted Iraqi artist Ismail Fattah al-Turk and carried through the various stages of detail design and working drawings by a group of young Iraqi architects all formed in the Baghdad School of Architecture. Kenneth Armitage, the internationally renowned sculptor, is said to have been so overwhelmed by it during a visit in 1986, that he hugged the artist in a fit of emotion quite uncharacteristic of an Englishman.[12]

The 'sculptural idea in the monument has been inspired by the principles of glorification of the "Martyr"', says the pamphlet issued on the opening day. But Saddam Husain's great war with Iran was in its first months when the monument was publicly announced, and had not yet enrolled all that many 'martyrs'. (The war began in September 1980 and on-site construction started in April 1981. The project would have been planned, drawn, managed and detailed many months before. Could it too, like the President's victory monument, actually have been conceived before the reality it commemorated, before the war had even started?) Shortly before he was put in jail for technical failures connected with the *Shaheed* Monument, over which he had no control (inexplicably, the specially made concrete paving slabs began curling up at the edges), Hisham al-Madfai, the Iraqi consulting engineer to the mayor on the project, wrote these words for opening day:

> In the era of the Leader-President, Saddam Husain, leader of the revolution and the people, the Iraqi Republic has achieved security of life for all Iraqis, so that they may enjoy honour, freedom and civilizational advance in all areas.

23

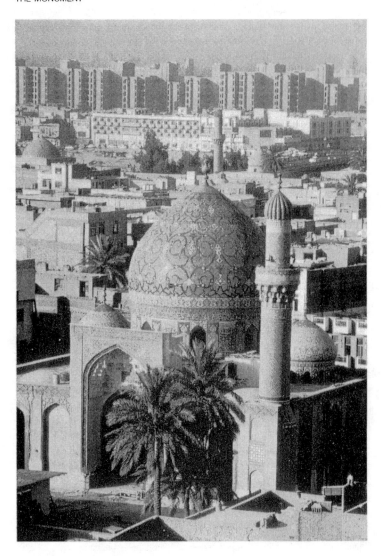

13. Looking towards new Haifa street across the old city.

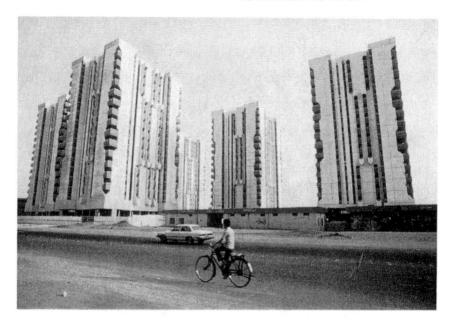

14. An exercise in alienation: 'post-modern' buildings of the 1980s mindlessly repeated in the worst traditions of 1950s town planning. The windows are supposed to have been derived from the *mashrabiyya*, a traditional lattice box-like screen usually projecting from an upper storey.

This memorial monument to our heroic martyrs has had great efforts, many competing brains and specializations poured into it, all so that it might signify this historical moment of Saddam's Iraq. Why, it even came into being under the guiding directions which spring from the heart of this foremost leader, and from his brain which is expansive enough to fit all the sons of Mesopotamia, those who are alive and those are eternal martyrs and will only come to life again in the arms of the Lord.[13]

A second enormous edifice of purely monumental import (obviously public buildings can also assume monumental significance but I am not here dealing with these) was built in tandem with the first and must have cost a great deal more. Unlike *Shaheed* which succeeds in creating an abstract, yet powerful and evocative symbolism by its use of the split dome, the 'Unknown Soldier' monument on July 14th street is simpleminded in the extreme (Figs. 17, 18). The tilted

25

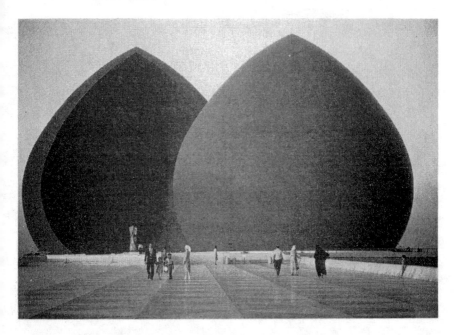

15. The *Shaheed* (Martyrs') Monument, 1983. Conceived by the Iraqi artist Ismail Fattah. A powerful new symbolism to commemorate the Iraqi dead in the Iraq - Iran war, created by slicing vertically through a traditional onion-profile dome clad in turquoise-blue ceramic tile (yet untraditionally 40 metres high). The twisted metal object in the centre is a three-dimensional flag (see Fig. 43).

behemoth, which looks like a flying saucer made from reinforced concrete and frozen in mid flight, represents a traditional shield — a *dira'a* — dropping from the dying grasp of the archetypal Iraqi warrior. No one, Iraqi or otherwise, sees the imagery in quite this way. And even when you are told what to look for, credulity is strained. This second major edifice was conceived by Khalid al-Rahal, to whose experience Saddam Husain would later turn.

Monuments like *Shaheed* and the Unknown Soldier, along with the scale of the physical changes in the urban fabric, did not completely escape the attention of the world. In 1985, for instance, the *National Geographic* published a photographic essay entitled 'The New Face of Baghdad', and in 1988 the Arabic daily, *Al-Hayat*, ran an article on how excellent it was to see the Iraqi sculptor moving 'from the atelier to the street'.[14] On the more sober professional front, a prominent

26

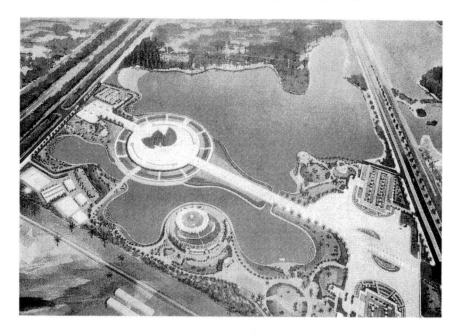

16. Artist's impression of whole project as published in the pamphlet *Nasb Shuhadaa Qadisiyyat Saddam* – issued by Amanat al-Asima (the Baghdad municipal authority).

Japanese architectural journal compared what was going on in Baghdad in the 1980s to Haussmann's late nineteenth-century reconstruction of Paris carried out under Napoleon III (in the relatively short span of twenty years, the journal stresses). The editor went on to suggest in the leading article that Baghdad had become a major urban testing ground for a new 'post-modern' aesthetic:

> Between 1979 and 1983, architects of the second and third generations of International Architecture gathered in Baghdad from all over the world to participate in the reconstruction and reorganization projects for the city. We could say it was a gathering of the most avant-garde ... These professionals were well aware of the kind of social and historical problems ... with which architecture was beset. They seemed to share an understanding of architecture and the age in which they live. In a broad sense, they had arrived in time

27

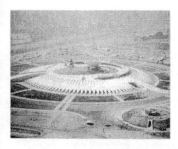

17. The Unknown Soldier Monument, 1982. Conceived by Khalid al-Rahal.

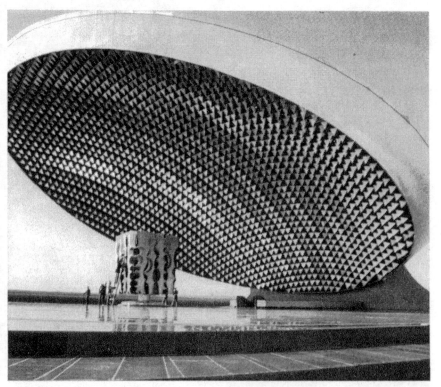

18. The tilted oval represents a traditional *dira'a* (Iraqi shield) and the ziggurat off to one side is a reference to the minaret of Samarra, one of the earliest and most famous minarets in Islamic architecture. There is a museum underground. Why? Because in order to hold up such an extraordinary cantilever in reinforced concrete, enormous foundations are needed. So why not?

to see the closing scenes of the Modern Architecture performance and were searching for a way out.

... President Saddam Husain has a clear image of what Baghdad should be like in the future [like Napoleon III]. He participated personally in some of the seminars which were held in Baghdad to debate architectural styles and policy. His personal participation has thus given an official backing to the overall revitalization of the city.

Consequently, some of Baghdad's architectural achievements ... reflect a clear sense of history and regionalism rooted in the history, climate and geographical location of the city. They are the potential source of a new global architectural movement. They also have the possibility of being refined into a style which could be called the true Baghdad Style, a particular architectural mode. They are in Chadirji's words [counsellor to the mayor on planning and architecture]: '... something arrived at, having gone through the process of the regionalization of International Architecture.'[15]

Shortly after the completion of *Shaheed* and the Unknown Soldier, the President conceived the third monument which is the focus of our study: the Victory Arch. The three monuments clearly form a unit. All refer to the gruelling eight-year war and the collective experience its pain and suffering forged in Iraq. But they do so in different ways. In Saddam Husain's final creation, I believe, the true conditions of monumentality as defined by Giedion, Leger and Sert are met. The President's monument is capable of haunting Iraqi memories and scratching at the psyche of all human beings in ways that even Fattah's overwhelming dome is not, much less Rahal's white elephant, although both are bigger, more deeply rooted in the ground (with concrete basements, exhibitions and all), and cost a great deal more to build. It exudes an ineffable special quality which is not shared with the two colossal monuments that preceded it, but is possessed by another curious and relatively modest scheme recently opened in the city of Basra.

In a green park on the banks of the corniche facing the Shatt al Arab waterway, framed by a silhouette of construction cranes and set amidst a surreal landscape of black billboards which remind visitors how many Iraqis died fighting for Basra and Faw and how many shells landed on Iraqi soil, are eighty lifesize and lifelike sculptures of officers and commanders who fell in those battles. This was a priority project in the frenzied post-war rush to rebuild virtually from scratch the pulverized cities of Basra and Faw. Made from real family

29

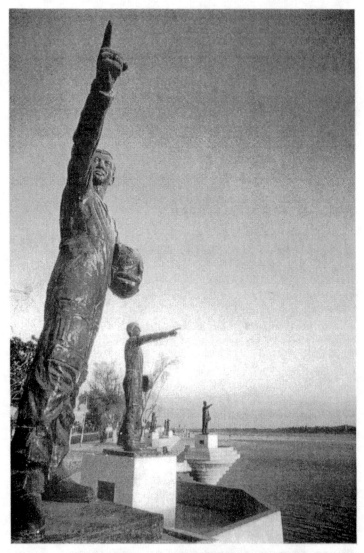

19. Sculpture park on the corniche, Basra. Iraqi officers point towards Iran across the most heavily fought over waterway in living memory. Eighty figures in all, sculpted from photographs of the dead men, 1989.

snapshots by a collective of Iraqi sculptors, they depict those heroes in a variety of forms of dress, in combat gear or without. Only one thing is common to all: every man's gaze is sternly fixed on the Iranian shore across the Shatt, and each has an arm accusingly stretched out pointing in the same direction (Fig. 19).

If there is such a thing as a particular aesthetic 'mode' in Saddam Husain's city (and I think there is), then the latest monument in the Baghdad series and the eerie surreal landscape in Basra are its apogee. Such forms and images bestow meaning upon that mode in the very specific conditions of Iraqi culture, history and politics. The President's 'Baghdad Style', not the early modernism transplanted from the West, nor the latest 'post-modern' aesthetic gymnastics of all those who so enthusiastically participated in the redevelopment of Baghdad, truly celebrates the Ba'thist city.[16]

Is monumentality an objective quality inherent in an urban community which is simply made manifest by the gifted artist, as the devotees of modernism have long assumed? Or is it merely an artist's eclectic interpretation of how the values and forms of his city might re-enact some tenets of culture or history, as the post-modernists would claim? Who comes first, the artist or the city? From the standpoint of this debate, Saddam Husain's monument is set apart from its precursors in being a concrete physical intervention in the city by the man who is behind all the other changes. (Likewise, although the Basra landscape is the pooled effort of many sculptors, it was inspired by one imagination, probably Saddam Husain's.) Hence, its creation momentarily dissolves a dichotomy which has plagued all those who have reflected on the city; it might even shed light on the general nature of monumentality itself.

The monument, Aldo Rossi wrote, 'is the sign upon which one reads something that cannot otherwise be said, for it belongs to the biography of the artist and the history of society'.[17] Rossi thought of monuments as fixed references within the city, itself conceived as a collective human artefact changing through time and made of many parts. For him as for Sert, Leger and Giedion, those three masters of modernism, monuments are those parts of the city imbued with persistence and permanence, a result of their capacity to encapsulate the history, art and collective memory of a place. They are works of art in their own right and 'more than' art in that they are signs of a collective will. The often repeated organic metaphor that likens the city to a biological organism whose form is constituted by evolutionary incremental adaptations to function, is rejected by Rossi. Instead, the monument is a special kind of work of art within an even larger work of art: the city. It is both a public event and a form identified with a 'style', unique in time and place, yet linking the city's past with its future. Always, therefore, the essence of a monument, like that of a city, lies in its destiny.

Rossi was thinking of Rome, Paris, Granada and great urban artefacts like the Roman Forum and the Alhambra; he did not have the new face of Baghdad and Saddam Husain's monument in mind. His way of thinking, however, reminds us that cities and their most genuine monuments are always mirror images of one another; inside the belly of the one you can untangle the meaning of the other. Saddam Husain's new Baghdad is not merely a run-of-the-mill Third World capital, haphazardly stuffed with people and ugly or beautiful artefacts as the case may be; it is also a collective state of mind which has its gods. Thinking about the meaning of these gods must remain as incomplete as the unfulfilled destiny of the Victory Arch itself.

Throughout history, the human being has always looked beyond what could be seen. However, sometimes we find that this trait makes him deal with the visible as though it existed outside his will and outside the objective presence of his senses. He turns the stone idol which he makes with his own hands into a god, in spite of the fact that this idol in its very material is from the same earth upon which he stands and labours. Therefore, the need of the human being to look beyond what lies between his hands, or to the 'spirit' of what is visible, is a real human need. It explains why the human being sometimes turns his stone idols into 'spirits'.

Frequently, this very knowledge and control over the visible turns into a need to look over the horizon, beyond what can be seen; it is exacerbated as his very pleasure with the visible keeps on building up until he feels bloated with all that he might require of material things to the point of suffocation and emptiness brought on by this material fulfilment . . .

Only after he has climbed the highest peaks do you find the human being looking beyond the horizon, and even higher.

Saddam Husain[18]

4
Politics
as Art

The activity of politics and the activity of art have the same relationship to life when looked at in the above way. Imagine the two ends of one measuring stick. At one end, missionary politics (in the sense of making 'the new man' and moulding 'the new society') is like art in that it is about action with an eye towards new forms. At the other extreme, what we know as democratic politics — understood as compromise, contradiction, complexity and the toleration of difference — is by its very nature submission to pre-existent forms. Both are 'ideal' types, which do not exist purely in the world, but simply help us to make real distinctions in concrete situations (pure

tolerance equals inaction; pure idealism admits no obstacle). Even
Saddam Husain has to tolerate others to some degree.

For art and for politics-as-art 'the world is but a thing of
appearances' which has to be brought into line with the artist's own
universe of logical Gestalt-formations.[19] Acting upon the world to
reshape its objectivity gathers art and politics together under a
uniquely human umbrella. Unlike science, which looks towards an
outer reality, the realism of art and politics-as-art is of their own
making; and both are profoundly idealistic because the reality they
create is a product of the mind. By eschewing submission for action,
every hope-filled political activist and all true artists are at one in their
relation to the world.

The only difference between Saddam Husain and the rest of us is
that like the better kind of artist he carries these traits to extraordinary
and fascinating extremes. The observation of Sert, Leger and Giedion
that 'as a rule, those who govern and administer a people, brilliant as
they may be in their special fields, represent the average man of our
period in their artistic judgements', does not apply to this President.[20]
They are at the other end of the measuring stick from Saddam Husain.
Even though his raw material is real people, not building materials or a
sheet of stretched canvas and paint, his imaginative impulses recognize
no limits. His freedom to create recognizes no one else's 'rights' (the
idea of the inviolability of the individual – as against the 'higher'
interest of the group – has never had any currency in Iraqi culture). In
fact like an artist, Saddam Husain's freedom is constrained only from
the inside, by the self-imposed and inbuilt limitations of his own
imagination and priorities. Therefore the criteria to judge him by have
to be those set by him, not those of a stranger, imposed from the
outside. Think of the view from the mountain top – cold, awesome,
inspiring. Think how inexplicable and dull nature's beauty would be
without it. Is it sensible to judge that view from the rubble at the
bottom? Saddam Husain's monument provides us with a view from
such a mountain top; it is a view into what we are capable of as a
species when we really put our minds to it. From its vantage point the
opportunity to re-ask old questions which may not have firm answers,
is spread out before our eyes.

In the moment of reflection quoted above, this artist-President is
providing us with a genuine human and historical insight. He is talking

about creation in art and politics, the act of making something out of nothing, or out of oneself, which is then imposed upon the world. Before the Renaissance this power could only be attributed to God. Michelangelo was the first artist to be called divine because to be as creative as that, people thought, you had to be divine. Thus, the idea of creativity as a human attribute came into being. Over time the modern notion took root that all men (and, later, women) were born with the potential to be creative, although some were more so than others in different fields. Whether or not the world was created in seven days, being creative was henceforth indissolubly bound up with human expression, self-realization, and the freedom to act upon that world with a view to reshaping it. The application of this attribute to politics and culture was the great achievement of the French Revolution. From these origins came the secular notions of artistic creation that we all now use and the view of politics as art which Saddam Husain was expounding to his biographer. Curiously, however, the President's monument takes us back to the idea of the divinity of the artist, stopping short of the idea of the artistry of the divine. Yet in its celebration of victory and in the physicality of its expression (the casting technique particularly) it is about modern man acting politically upon the world, free of all encumbrances. All in all, therefore, one might see it as the crystallization into physical form of combined and uneven developments in the history of ideas about art and politics.

The words the President is using, however, should not be viewed as absolute truths. He would not view them that way himself. They are as relative as the history of ideas we have just been considering. The President is talking about himself. Always our views of human nature — be they those of the grandest philosophers or the most humble or tyrannical of persons — are taken from our own experiences and privately arrived at view of the world. They tell as much about temperament and character as they do about 'truth'. Nonetheless to the extent that they are said in good faith they will possess a degree of human objectivity because temperament and character are also constitutive of 'truth'. Pushed to it, we can all find something in such words — something that is true about a friend, or was even true about ourselves for a while. Such a moment of recognition is a link that binds us even to someone like Saddam Husain. Beyond that initial link we might also surmise in Husain's philosophizing an overweening ambition, and a feverish restlessness with regards to achievement. Still, nothing wrong with that.

But the strange thing is that this president quite literally does not stop at anything. Always he is driven feverishly forward, confronting and if necessary obliterating anything and everything that stands in his way. Like some allegorical type, he seems not to have acquired his character, but been born into it (his name, *saddam*, means in Arabic 'the one who confronts', or 'who smashes through obstacles'). In power, this president, unlike the run-of-the-mill politician or activist, wanted and got everything. When he said that even the 'writing of Arab history' must 'be from our [Ba'thist] point of view with an emphasis on analysis [i.e. form] and not realistic storytelling [i.e. content]', he made it happen in the Iraq of the 1970s and 1980s.[21]

In true Platonic form, however, his view of politics is best summed up in his thoughts on education. In an important speech addressed to a mass meeting of the employees of the Ministry of Education chastizing them for their shortcomings as educators, Saddam Husain said:

> You must get at adults through their sons, in addition to other means. Teach the student to object to his parents if he hears them discussing state secrets ... You must place in every corner a son of the revolution, with a trustworthy eye and a firm mind that receives its instructions from the responsible centre of the revolution ... Also teach the child to beware of the foreigner, for the latter is a pair of eyes for his country and some of them are saboteurs of the revolution ... The child in his relationship to the teacher is like a piece of raw marble in the hands of a sculptor who has the power to impart aesthetic form, or discard the piece to the ravages of time and the vagaries of nature.[22]

The character of this man and his view of politics converge in his manner of thinking an art object into existence. He relates to a child as an artist relates to his or her raw material. Artistic creation, while it is still going on, is as relentlessly dynamic, repetitive, confrontational, contradictory and difficult as this kind of utopian politics. Both resemble life in its tempestuous and difficult moments. Once created, however, the work of art is harmless thought frozen in time and fixed in sensual shape; it is dead thought. It has acquired the quality of duration, of timelessness, but at the expense of action, at the expense of life. The same cannot be said of the outcome of Saddam Husain's kind of education, insofar as Saddam Husain's child still retains human attributes. To the extent that the ability to act, and hence to be human, is lost in a child educated in Saddam Husain's regime, the analogy holds. In the child, not in the monument, we come up against the real rub of politics, the point at which it ought perhaps to diverge from art even though it doesn't always do so.

Political action can have constitutions, laws or new institutions as its end. These human artefacts are every bit as 'subjective' as a work of art. As a collective (nation or polity), we choose to want them, or we don't. But the real thrill of politics is not in such conventional and historically specific 'works'; it is in the activity of politics itself, as anyone who has tasted activism knows. The charge we get out of political activity is like the labour of Sisyphus; it operates at great risk and disappears the moment the activity ceases. Usually there is nothing at the end of the road except (in a democracy) the formal guarantee of being able to repeat the action itself, taste more of the pleasure of being Sisyphus, of permanently oscillating between the extremes of ecstasy and despair.

In acting publicly on a stage, I can 'find' myself, if so inclined. 'All the world's a stage,' said Shakespeare whose characters play out their infinitely nuanced destinies in such a spirit over and over again. One can also, it is true, enjoy the spectacle of public life passively like the audience in the theatre (an enjoyment that grows with age). But if a citizen is inclined to be political (not just think or write about politics like a voyeur), he or she will almost always want to perform on that stage again and again, until 'burned out' or too old for the game.

Which human passion is at the root of politics? The urge for sociality, thought Aristotle. Beneficence and love of one's fellow human beings, argued Rousseau in his searing indictment of the Enlightenment and the principle of 'reason' in politics which he believed elevated self-love over love-of-the-other. 'Nationalism is love before anything else,' wrote Michel 'Aflaq, the founder of the Ba'th party and Saddam Husain's early mentor in all things political. 'He who loves does not ask for reasons. And if he were to ask, he would not find them. He who cannot love except for a clear reason, has already had this love wither away in himself and die.'[23] The difficult problem, therefore, is to look at Saddam Husain's child in the

37

knowledge that 'like a piece of raw marble in the hands of a sculptor' he was sculpted in the white heat of such overbearing love.

The cynical view of politics (of politicians as inveterate liars, charlatans, cheats and double-dealers) is too superficial to explain such an enigma. Anyway, cynicism quickly turns into a holier-than-thou attitude, one which assumes the cynic is comfortably removed from the ugliness of it all. A polity like Iraq under Saddam Husain forges cynicism in thought and opportunism in deed as a sort of psychological rampart to ward off the engulfing embrace of too much love. But it is not itself forged that way. Politics-as-art or nationalism-as-love, two sides of the same coin, are the original facts of life in a country like Iraq. To say such things is not to criticize, or parody the way things are; it is the logical conclusion of taking the President's words (and his monument) seriously and at face value.

The only demarcation between artistic and political activity is that whereas the latter is always ephemeral, the former has a durable outcome: the art object imbued with aura, set apart from the mortality of its artist. Monuments provide the permanence (which Aldo Rossi likes to call 'persistence') that politics always lacks. Hitler, 'frustrated artist' that he obviously was, understood this better than any other politician of the twentieth century. He had taken to sketching monuments for the city of Berlin in the early 1920s, at the time of the great inflation when there was hardly a shred of hope that he would ever come to power (Fig. 20). Albert Speer, the young architect appointed to carry out his plans after 1933, thought Hitler's 'sense of political mission and his passion for architecture were always inseparable'.[24] Speer tells an amusing story in this regard concerning a 'Theory of Ruin Value' which he developed for Hitler's benefit.

Modern construction methods, Speer thought in 1933, were 'poorly suited to form that "bridge of tradition" to future generations which Hitler was calling for'. Rusting heaps of rubble were not heroic enough; they didn't age nicely and were incapable of inspiring the lofty sentiments that Gothic cathedrals had so inspired in John Ruskin, for instance.[25] Speer's theory dealt with this problem of modern detritus in a host of technical and constructional ways. To illustrate his ideas he had a drawing prepared which showed what a building would look like

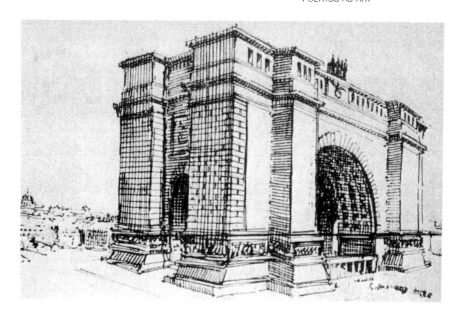

20. Hitler's 1925 sketch of a triumphal arch intended as a monument to Germans killed in World War I. Derived from the Arc de Triomphe but greatly enlarged.

after generations of neglect, overgrown with ivy, its columns fallen, the walls crumbling here and there, but the outlines still clearly recognizable. In Hitler's entourage this drawing was regarded as blasphemous. That I could even conceive of a period of decline for the newly founded Reich destined to last a thousand years seemed outrageous to many of Hitler's closest followers. But he himself accepted my ideas as logical and illuminating. He gave orders that in the future the important buildings of his Reich were to be erected in keeping with the principles of this 'law of ruins'.[26]

From the standpoint of politics-as-art, therefore, the most fundamental significance of Saddam Husain's monument is that like Hitler's forty metres high triumphal arch (also two and a half times the height of its Parisian inspiration), it reifies his personal joy in politics, a joy which under Iraqi conditions happens to be exclusively restricted to him and which in the nature of things can only end at his death. The price for the freezing of any 'idea' into fixed and permanent form is always the vibrancy and everchanging sensually experienced nature of life itself. In a different way the children of the Ba'th also pay this price. And that price once paid, the 'living spirit' of an artist, a period, or even a whole people at a particular point in their history, can only survive in the unfeeling permanence of an artefact. The wonderful thing is that great monuments are proof that sometimes it does.

To see a World in a Grain of Sand
And a Heaven in a Wild Flower,
Hold Infinity in the palm of your hand
And Eternity in an hour.

                William Blake[27]

5
Andy Warhol
and Saddam Husain

When Andy Warhol silkscreened a Campbell's soup can from a photographic enlargement, he made a statement about art and popular culture deemed worthy of New York's finest museums and most prestigious art galleries (Fig. 21). The ordinariness of a mass-produced consumer good was played off against the aura of a work of art. The idea was: 'You all may think you have seen a Campbell's soup can many times before, but this canvas is saying you haven't *really seen* it.'

Much as Americans experience in daily life a ubiquitous culture of consumerism and advertising, Iraqis experience the awesome power of their leader. Pictures in homes, posters in every shop, restaurant and public building, larger-than-life painted cutouts draped along avenues,

41

streets and squares, to say nothing of the Leader's continuous presence
on radio and television in an endless variety of calculated poses and
costumes — these are the signs, neon lights, advertisements, billboards
and television commercials of modern life in the city of Baghdad
(Figs. 22–25). They work on the mind subliminally, behind the scenes
as it were; and they are taken for granted because at first they had to
be, and today nobody can afford to remember how it all started or
recall the 'old times' when it used to be so different. People forget and
repetition breeds new habits; gradually what was in the forefront of
awareness slips down into more mysterious recesses.

In spite of the media and the flood of images, visually the public has
not yet experienced the authority of their President in quite the way
demanded by the new monument. The issue here is not one of mere
remembrance; unlike the clutter of surrounding images, it brings one
face to face with the overriding reality, forcing it suddenly to the
surface of awareness. Over time, all other conditions remaining the
same, such a monument to victory and the authority of Saddam
Husain may acquire even greater 'aura' by virtue of this perfect fit
between intention, physical form and the corresponding reality. It
would not do for Saddam Husain to have his arm improved upon by
an artist-technician, any more than it would do for Andy Warhol to
modify on canvas by his own brush strokes Campbell's original design
of their soup can. (Jasper Johns, Warhol's predecessor, had already
done that in his 1960 hand-painted pair of bronze beer cans. Johns
deliberately did not reproduce the labels or the dimensions of the cans
exactly; he 'reworked' them in small ways.) Transferring the literal
image using a photograph, with all that this implies about illusion
versus reality, illustration or art, was essential to the artistic moment of
Warhol's work. And it is essential to the art in Saddam Husain's
monument.

Frankly, the art objects of Andy Warhol and Saddam Husain's
monument leave me cold. The former is harmless, which cannot be
said of the latter, but this is something else entirely. The experience of
a work of art is after all morally neutral. Why shouldn't the world of
consumer goods and market relations touch modern people in the
same exquisite way that William Blake's grains of sand and wild
flowers touched their nineteenth-century counterparts? And who can
dismiss the pride that many ordinary Iraqis certainly feel as they look

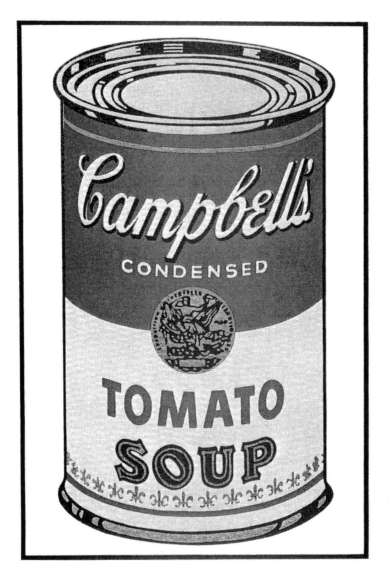

21. Campbell's Soup Can, Andy Warhol, 1964. Silkscreen on canvas, 35³/₄ x 24 ins.

up in wonder at the symbol of a great national ordeal overcome (in excess of ten per cent of the population are party members, and proportionally as many Iraqis died in the Iraq–Iran war as Britons in World War I)? Nonetheless, whatever we may feel about the efforts of Warhol and Husain (whether we 'like' them or not), both end up posing the question 'what is art?', and in similar ways. This is the source of their endless fascination.

Warhol's art is not intended as satire, parody, or any other critical or 'elitist' form of social commentary. 'Pop Art is liking things,' said Andy Warhol; and Roy Lichtenstein, the Pop artist famous for his cartoon and comic strip enlargements, reacted to how his work was received by saying: 'The things that I have apparently parodied, I actually admire.' Claes Oldenburg is for an art that is as 'sweet and stupid as life itself'.[28] People saw what they were looking for in Warhol whose adamant refusal to comment captured something real in the American post-war experience. Even in his Death and Disaster series (depicting electric chairs and plane wrecks), Warhol was content to gaze at the horrors of modern life as though viewing a TV soap opera. How different this all was from the reforming zeal and utopianism of early moderns like the Futurists and Constructivists!

In the end, Warhol's work and career translate an acceptance of commercialism into images which were true to many of the values Americans grew up with:

> Not everyone is so apathetic that he will watch a rape or murder without acting to prevent it, but many are. Most of us are unmoved by the public and private disasters that touched and enraged artists and thinkers in the 1930s. After World War II the tear glands of the world dried up from over-use. It is this world for which Warhol is spokesman.[29]

Warhol pursued this throughout all the stages of his career until finally he changed the way in which we see the world. He made art more completely complicit in the prevailing culture of its production than any other artist of this century. The idea that art could or should aspire to reach beyond its original confines became deeply problematic. In the face of this radical relativism and subjectivism, the universal language of line, form, volume and colour in which artists had hitherto 'spoken' to one another, began to decline in influence.

Following the logic of his point of view and after becoming an

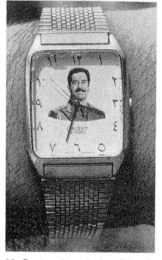

22. Peering through the dials of a gold wristwatch

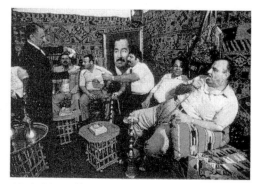

23. Inside a café

24. Presiding over a peasant dwelling in Shi'ite marsh region of southern Iraq

25. A billboard in the desert

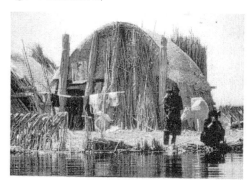

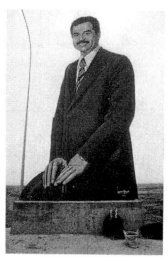

45

overnight success, Warhol set up an 'art factory', churning out portraits of the wives of rich collectors. From painting images to silkscreening photographs to making films about sexual life-styles, to becoming a night-club owner and rock musician, Warhol ended up realizing the enormous business potential of being himself (to the point of putting out a gossip magazine called *Andy Warhol's Interview*). In this he presaged the whole contemporary rock 'superstar' phenomenon. As another admirer put it, there 'would have been no "glitter" without Warhol, Mick Jagger would have remained a blues shouter, David Bowie would not have happened at all'.[30] Quite aside from the issue of 'harmfulness' or otherwise of a work of art, therefore, a remarkable structural correspondence exists between Warhol and Saddam Husain's work in relation to their respective societies: both succeed in elevating uncritical acceptance of public reality to the point of deification. And both became heroes in their own lifetimes by adhering to given values, not by criticizing them.

My objection to the art by itself (in isolation from its later fusion into the persona of the artist) is not that it is uncritical. Art can glorify as well as criticize; often it simply describes with nuance and feeling. My objection is that Warhol's pictures are too verbal, too intellectualized. They eschew visual perception for abstraction of a non-visual nature. The imagery is ruled by an idea which can be communicated in words. The picture itself is often simply an illustration of the words (this is how things work in commercial advertising agencies where Warhol worked for many years before striking out on his own as an artist).

The same objection, incidentally, is construed as a source of 'greatness' by the historian-philosopher, Michel Foucault. He sees Warhol not as a painter, but as one of this century's great inventors of 'acategorical thought'. Categories 'instruct us in the ways of knowledge and solemnly alert us to the possibilities of error ... Thus, we court danger in wanting to be freed from categories; no sooner do we abandon their organizing principle than we face the magma of stupidity.' Which is precisely what Warhol did, according to Foucault, with his constant blurring of fixed boundaries like the separation of art from advertising, beauty from vulgarity, the profound from the superficial, or the artist from the rock star. Stupidity says: 'What difference if the colours vary, if they're darker or lighter. It's all so senseless — life, women, death! How ridiculous this stupidity!' Warhol faces up to stupidity (unlike the rest of us who like to hold on to categories and distinctions) and in an inspired flash realizes that the only thing left, the only thing that counts any longer is 'multiplicity itself — with nothing at its center, at its highest point, or beyond it'.[31] The soup can becomes the levelling uniformity of many soup cans, the Marilyn Monroe portrait becomes the infinite undifferentiated extension of mass culture. And so on.

Thus the language of vision — of forms and colours which have to be seen, not talked about, to be experienced — is abolished. The separate capacity for concrete perceiving, for learning how to look (as music is learning how to hear) has been replaced by the capacity for abstract thinking (the tools of Foucault's trade). And this is the outcome irrespective of whether one 'likes' Warhol's art or not.

But if Warhol has succeeded in blurring boundaries and destroying distinctions, then surely so has Saddam Husain. What is his monument? Is it art? Is it kitsch? Is it vulgar? Is it beautiful? Is it good or is it bad? Can we even afford to remain indifferent towards it? Does 'liking' or 'not liking' it have anything to do with our answers to such questions? And suppose we are citizens of the city in which this monument occupies pride of place. Does that make a difference? It is so much easier to wash away Warhol's soup can in the endless ocean of his relativism, indifference and 'acategorical thought' than it is Saddam Husain's monument.

Then there are other problems. After all, turning the ready-made object into art, or into a question about art (Is it art, or is it a Campbell soup can?) had been done before (by Marcel Duchamp, for instance, at the beginning of the twentieth century). After Duchamp, Warhol is boring. Such statements about art can only be made once. Once made, the image on canvas is as discardable as the soup can depicted. Warhol's cans forgo the uniqueness imparted by time. They look like every other Campbell's soup can; they have no character. There is no entirely independent level of purely visual thinking going on — employing the old-fashioned painterly qualities of line, colour, form, texture. Intellectual content has taken over from visual rendition. The point of *painting*, of labouring over the relation of brush stroke to visual form, is lost. With too many Warhols around, the purely seen dimension of what is after all still one of the *visual* arts will become even more impoverished. The canvas is intellected; it does not reveal its charms slowly, over many viewings, by an active perceptual effort on the part of the viewer. But then that is the whole point and Warhol's claim to fame lies in being one of the many twentieth-century subverters of his own profession. New art forms rise (collage, photography, assemblage, cinema, computer graphics) and old ones are done away with from within, at least for a while.

For Iraqis, and from a purely artistic point of view, the question is: Do they experience their own world in ways that Saddam Husain, in an inspired instant, like Andy Warhol, managed to capture in a meaningful way? Does the form match the intention and build on already accepted values, thereby freezing into bronze and for all time a truth about their world that many Iraqis recognize? For the briefest of moments snatched out of a busy wartime schedule, Saddam Husain thought like an artist. The fact that, like Warhol, he was both the subject and object of his own reflections is a common enough occurrence among artists.

The casino in Las Vegas is big, low space. It is the archetype for all public interior spaces ... We have replaced the monumental space of Pennsylvania Station by a subway above ground, and that of Grand Central Terminal remains mainly through its magnificent conversion to an advertising vehicle. Thus ... our money and skill do not go into the traditional monumentality that expressed cohesion of the community through big-scale, unified, symbolic architectural elements. Perhaps we should admit that ... apart from theaters and ball parks, the occasional communal space that is big is a space for crowds of anonymous individuals without explicit connection with each other. The big, low mazes of the dark restaurant with alcoves combine being together and yet separate as does the Las Vegas casino. The lighting in the casino achieves a new monumentality for the low space. The controlled sources of artificial and colored light within the dark enclosures expand and unify the space ... You are no longer in the bounded piazza but in the twinkling lights of the city at night.

Robert Venturi et al.[32]

6
Vulgarity
and Art

Unfortunately for the President, the extraordinary vulgarity of his metaphor for victory over Iran spoils the imaginative punch of the decision to cast, rather than model, the arms. The potential 'beauty' of this way of making is lost in a maze of unintended contradictions and formal weaknesses.

To begin with, the decision to duplicate the arch at either end of the parade grounds was crass (Figs. 26, 27). The first sketch (see Fig. 3) shows that this was the President's intention from the beginning. Duplication suggests that there is more than one way of entering and leaving such a place. This is not in the spirit of the city to which the monument belongs, as Saddam Husain should have realized. Nor does

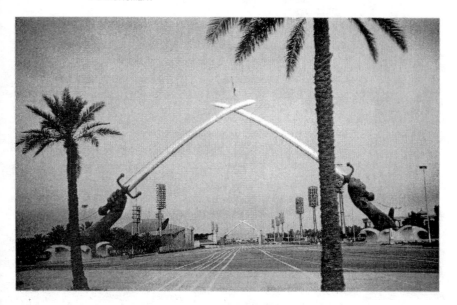

26. The Monument viewed along the ceremonial axis and showing both arches. Note the gigantic ultra-modern football stadium lights along the route and the bizarre tortoise-shell structure of the viewing stand on the left. Yet another example of the visual schizophrenia typical of the Ba'thist city. See in this regard Fig. 6.

the duality correspond to classical principles of planning in this part of the world: the individual three-dimensional gateway is a vital element in both ancient Mesopotamian and Islamic architecture (Fig. 28). Moreover, physically reproducing the identical pair of arms in the same pose twice, deflates the value of each as a monument. It no longer matters very much how good a sculpture of Lenin is, for example, if one ends up finding it in every Russian town and city centre. The aura of uniqueness imparted by casting the artist-President's arms is diminished, undermining the singularity of the statement (a variation on a similar theme for the other arch would have been better).

The scale too seems to have gone completely awry. It is not that the monument is too big; on the contrary, from one point of view too little of the forearms has been used. The problem is one of relative proportion and scaling down to the human what is anyway going to be enormous; it is not a problem of sheer size. The arms are much too

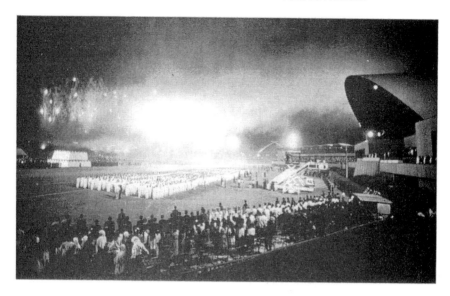

27. The viewing stand, ceremonial axis and fireworks at night. The Victory Arch can just be seen in the far distance: Nuremburg and Las Vegas rolled into one.

far apart to read as a pair (approximately ninety metres centre to centre). Yet they are supposed to form one arch. No attempt is made to unify them (through treatment of the ground for instance). As a consequence the arch is flat and thin, chopped through the middle by a massive highway, and taking its cue from the cheapest kind of billboard (Fig. 29). It lacks entirely that fundamental quality of all sculptural form: volume and three-dimensionality (a point highlighted by observing Henry Moore's magnificent arch in Hyde Park). A penetrable monument provides a rare sculptural opportunity because it is possible to explore from the inside as well as the outside. But the opportunity has been completely missed, as it is always missed in those plywood cutout arches hastily erected by local authorities in Third World cities for the edification of visiting dignitaries.[33]

What happens to a disembodied pair of forearms when they are enormously enlarged? The proportions of our bodies are so deeply ingrained in us that they cannot easily be escaped. Unless

51

disembodiment and scale transformation work to a new artistic purpose (within their own imagined reality, as in some surrealist works), the bodily standard will reimpose itself, as it does in the case of this monument. One cannot therefore avoid the desire to imagine the whole person of Saddam Husain gripping the two swords. But even if the President's body could be contorted into the appropriate position he would look ridiculously squat. (I estimate his shoulders would have to be three times their normal width.) The same problem repeats itself with the fists. In the film, 'Architecture of Fear', which tried to simulate through special effects how the swords were being held, the impossibility of twisting one's wrists into the appropriate position was practically demonstrated to those working it out.[34]

Another problem with such spectacular transformations of scale, is

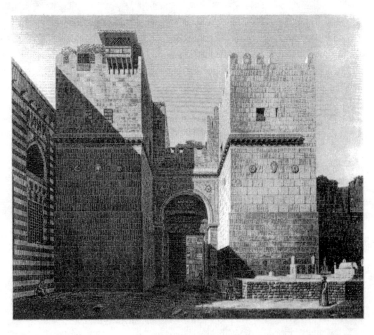

28. Bab al-Nasr (the gate of victory). One of Cairo's great gates as illustrated by Napoleon's architects when he invaded Egypt in 1798 (published in *Description de l'Egypte*). Note the seated and standing figures for a sense of the scale.

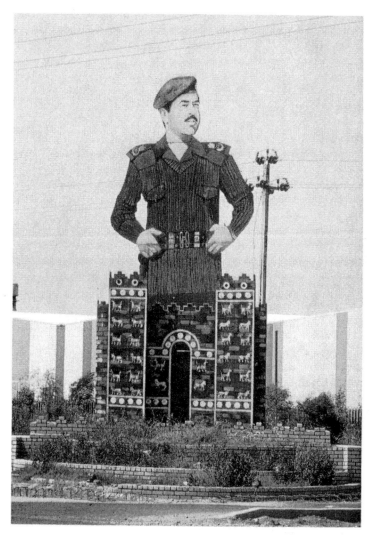

29. A giant plywood billboard representing Saddam Husain astride the ancient Babylonian gate of Ishtar. Quite apart from the imagery, the paper-thin flatness (in relation to size) of this construction makes it even more ridiculous than it need have been. The contrast with the majestic yet human three-dimensionality of Bab al-Nasr (Fig. 28) is evident. See also the Ishtar Gate in its reconstructed (half-size) version in Fig. 39.

that they affect our common-sense perception of the bodily standard itself. To 'feel' right at a given scale, it is necessary sometimes to distort proportions. Perspective artists know this. Baroque architects were constantly experimenting with the illusion of space because what concerned them was how a space is experienced emotionally, not how true it is to some principle or other (a typical concern of early modern architects). But can the forearms be deliberately distorted? How should the two ideas of casting and distortion be reconciled? Such questions are the bread and butter of an artist's professionalism, involving experience, knowledge, a cultivated imagination and a great deal of time-consuming experimentation. One thing can safely be assumed: although a great deal of money was spent on this monument, no one advised Saddam Husain about such considerations, or dared to take them into account on his behalf in the execution of the work.

Consider next the junction point of ground and aggressively sword-waving arms. The ideology tells us to expect some violent volcanic eruption out of the bowels of the earth scattering earth and debris in a triumphant ascent to the sky (see Fig. 2). Instead, a golden opportunity to thicken the stick-like quality of the arms at the base through the treatment of the ground over a much larger area has been wasted. Something that could be a tulip (anyway a flower of some kind) peels back its petals. These are not only made out of concrete, they are made to *look* as if they are made out of concrete. Out of this gentle centre, draped and studded with real Iranian helmets (which might as well have been human skulls from the point of view of the intention), his arms sprout (Fig. 30). Why are the helmets inside an inflated peanut bag, inexplicably described as a 'net'? Nets have no warrior-like connotations in Iraq. Why the switch of material to concrete when both arms and swords are in metal? Since the flag figured in the first speech announcing the scheme (see Fig. 3), why did it get tacked on in such a stupid way (Fig. 31)? Anyway it cannot be seen. Again, someone got the scale completely wrong. Was that an oversight? I don't think so. The problem with a flag at that kind of height is the wind. You can't keep on climbing up the swords to replace it. Anyway the pole is seven metres high. Should the flag itself not have been made of metal as in the Martyrs' Monument (see Fig. 43)?

The vulgarity of Saddam Husain's monument is physically

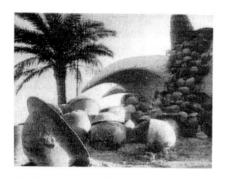

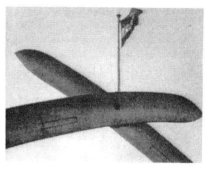

30. The concrete 'exploding ground' with 2,500 Iranian helmets pouring out of a torn peanut bag which can be seen rearing up in the background. The bag is made of bronze and has to be tied on to the grip of the sword with some sort of cable (presumably because it would be structurally unstable otherwise).

31. The tacked on flag, completely disproportionate in scale. Passing under the flag was always part of the original intention (see extract from Husain's speech of 1985, Fig. 3).

confirmed time and time again in the mindlessness of such details. Although the temptation is great, the biggest mistake a viewer or critic can make is to imagine that complex thoughts are buried in all this imagery. Almost certainly there are fascinating psychological insights to be gained from these 'slips', but from the visual standpoint, we cannot afford to lose sight of the fact that what we are dealing with here is sheer blinding inanity.

Unlike Andy Warhol, this artist-President has no ulterior intention of subverting the canons of artistic taste. His is not the anti-art of art (as Surrealism was anti-Cubism and Pop was anti-Abstract Expressionism); his is the art of popular taste which speaks directly and forcefully through symbols and signs, not through the inherent physiognomic characteristics of form and material or the complex interaction of carefully juxtaposed imagery. Visually the vulgarity of the statement as a whole is in the untransformed, purely literal quality of its symbolism (not in its aggressivity or the fact that it signifies victory through death, a common enough theme in the history of art). Saddam Husain's authority, which arose in complicated historical circumstances and derives from very large numbers of people, is signified too effortlessly, as a boring statement of transparent fact that does not require imaginative assimilation (just as his details do not

55

require critical explication once you realize that, like accidents, no thought went into them). All the subtleties of a way of making, of casting versus moulding or carving or assembling, are lost, just as they are lost in a building whose structural expression is covered up by applied decoration, or one whose form is a completely literal and singular translation of its function. Much of the so-called Pop architecture of Los Angeles or the Strip in Las Vegas – the casinos extolled by Robert Venturi – work in this way: gigantic decorated sheds tucked away behind their signs and appliqué glitter, or even completely merged into them; a hot dog stand in the shape of a giant hot dog, complete with mustard, that is actually used for selling hot dogs (Fig. 32). Imagine Saddam Husain solemnly designing this building in the name of great architecture and you have a perfect analogy with the monument.

The monument is certainly expressive, as expressive as the hot dog stand. But the emotions being expressed appear as pure subject matter,

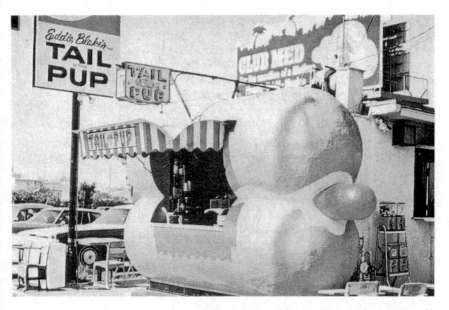

32. A hot-dog stand in Los Angeles. Form and symbolic intent meet here in a perfect analogy with Saddam Husain's monument.

surface psychology. Unlike those just as unsavoury emotions of the Marquis de Sade, for instance, they do not obey and enlarge on the dark forces of intuition and creativity which all good art relies upon when it wants to plumb the unknown depths of the human soul. The President is not plumbing any depths; he is not being moved by a sinful ardour to explore an aesthetic virtue.

Maybe 'vulgar' is the wrong word. Could the monument simply be an example of bad art? Quentin Bell says that 'bad art' is a form of insincerity, which results from 'social pressure in favour of that which society at large calls beauty'.[35] In the last one hundred years, he claims, the good artist has always fought against the popular conception of beauty while the bad artist has worked within its constraints. Naturally, the President thinks of himself as the creator of a great work of art, not a bad one. To this Bell retorts: 'The damnable thing about bad art is that the insincerity which lies at its roots is not perceived by the artist himself.'[36]

While this argument may be convincing in relation to the history of art, it falters in the face of the strange reality created by Saddam Husain. Towards whom is he insincere? Would it make a difference if he had studied art long and hard, or been the son of illustrious figures in the art world like Quentin Bell? Even then he could not be accused of insincerity to the principles he had studied, for he might be rejecting them like Andy Warhol. He might have a hidden sense of humour and be tweaking all our noses in the name of art; it has been done before and will be done again. The problem lies in the real intentions of Saddam Husain which cannot be wholly political or propagandistic because we can see at least one purely artistic moment in the monument: the decision to cast the artist-President's arms, a decision that is simply too perfect from the standpoint of form, material and matching intention, too impossible to improve upon given the problem and the reality that the artefact is addressing. However, only one artistic instance (I am unable to find another) inside the frame of a vulgar whole is not enough to turn vulgarity into art, not even into bad art.

In order to proceed it is necessary to suppose that the President's solemnity, his intentions as a monument maker, are not by and large artistic. Politics as art is *politics* not art; it is the discipline in which this President has vested time and effort. It is also a discipline in which, as we have seen, he has gained knowledge and reasonably profound insights into human nature. The monument is not about thinking from inside the establishment of art; it is about thinking like the maker of that giant hot dog stand who is more concerned with knowing his customers and selling them hot dogs than he is with fine art.

Vulgarity is not bad art, although in the President's monument it mimics it. To be vulgar is to be too direct, to flaunt intentionality without nuance. That is not always a bad thing to do. Vulgarity even has an appeal corresponding to its distance from hypocrisy and snobbery. Vulgarity and art, like populism and elitism, are separate but deeply intertwined. If the President's creation is vulgar, no amount of clever footwork regarding bad art will resolve its nature. You still have to be an artist in order to be a bad one. Yet, paradoxically, our prevailing conceptions of these two categories have been changing at such an accelerated pace, the distinction itself − between art and vulgarity (even between good and bad art) − is beginning to fall apart. The work of Robert Venturi, probably the most influential post-modern architect, powerfully illuminates the increasingly complex relation between art and vulgarity so characteristic of our times.

In the spirit of Pop art, Venturi reacted against the *tabula rasa* reductivism of the Modern Movement in built form. He rejected ideas of pure form, anti-ornamentalism, consistency, harmony and unconventional technology, in favour of mixed media, regionalism, symbolism, applied ornament, popular iconography, expedient architecture, inconsistency, and conventional technology. 'The main justification for honky-tonk elements in architectural order', he wrote in 1966, 'is their very existence. They are what we have. Architects can bemoan or try to ignore them or even try to abolish them, but they will not go away. Or they will not go away for a long time because architects do not have the power to replace them (nor do they know what to replace them with).' Conventional elements (from copings to cornices to windows and commercial display signs) should be made more vivid, and used in ways that did not shun the inconsistencies, disharmonies and eclecticism that would result. 'Through unconventional organization of conventional parts [the architect] is able to create new meanings within the whole. If ... he organizes familiar things in an unfamiliar way, he is changing their contexts, and he can use even the cliché to gain a fresh effect.'[37]

What began as a populist, unpretentious and even witty way of highlighting real limitations of the profession (along with rejecting the elitism and messianic idealism of Le Corbusier, Mies van der Rohe and Frank Lloyd Wright), turned into something else with *Learning from Las Vegas*, first published in 1972 (Fig. 33). Venturi was moving from 'complexity and contradiction', towards positive discovery of hitherto unperceived aesthetic qualities in, for instance, the neon signs and symbols along the Strip in Las Vegas. The messy, commercialized and eclectic hodge-podge of Main Street, USA, was, in Venturi's famous phrase, 'almost all right'. Casinos were oases which replaced traditional monuments, and billboards did not litter the landscape, they 'beautified' it.[38]

This is the language of Andy Warhol in architecture. But Venturi went beyond Warhol in that he sought to justify 'the symbolism of the ugly and ordinary'.[39] He liked calling his designs ugly and ordinary. The canons of beauty and taste were being overturned. The hot dog stand, like the stone chapel of an Italian hill town, had become an object of admiration from which professional architects could learn something. Modern architecture, which had so sneered at popular iconography, started to give way to those it had disinherited. Venturi became the most interesting anti-architect of modern architecture.

In the light of Venturi, something happens to the vulgarity of Saddam Husain's monument. Does it go away? No. But according to his rules, it should. Why doesn't it go away? The problem is that after Warhol and Venturi, no one can answer such questions with certainty. However, we are able to consider the same problem from a slightly

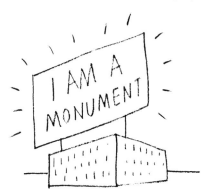

33. Robert Venturi's recommendation for a monument

different angle. In the light of the monument, what happens to Venturi's aesthetic?

In 1983, Venturi, by now a major star in the architectural firmament, was invited by Saddam Husain to participate in one of the grandest architectural competitions ever sponsored in a country of the Third World. The reader will recall that Baghdad had become a testing ground for massive urban renewal. The brief was for a State Mosque, the jewel in the crown of the whole redevelopment programme. A galaxy of famous names was invited. The project was initiated in the third year of the Iraq—Iran war, at a time when it had become obvious that this was no ordinary war, and Iraq could not achieve its original aims in starting it. Nonetheless, an Islamic revolution across the border had to be fought on many fronts at the same time.

The new mosque was intended to symbolize the religious, state and national beliefs of the people of Iraq, and the President emphasized that the final design should represent 'a leap forward in the art of architecture'.[40] The programme called for the biggest continuous indoor prayer hall area in the world (for 30,000 persons, along with nonceremonial daily prayer areas), an enormous library, a teaching institute, conference facilities, accommodation for forty visiting imams, and many other things beside. A three-day televised symposium, convened by the President, and attended by every available Iraqi professional and senior government official, was held in Baghdad to hear the architects, debate the entries and announce the results. Quite apart from the architecture, the competition was an orchestrated event of national proportions.

In its wisdom, the Mayor's office saw fit to publish all the submissions. Minoru Takeyama, a Japanese post-modernist and winner of numerous prizes, had done some homework. He took the circular plan of al-Mansur's original city (of which not a trace is left) as a 'frame' and the plan of the Great Mosque of Samarra as the 'spirit' of a scheme imbued with historical references. These he jammed into one another (Fig. 34). The Spanish architect, Ricardo Bofill, produced a melange of many Mesopotamian building traditions, organized along a ceremonial axis. To him, architectural form is created by 'rummaging in the world of history', not Las Vegas, and blending the result 'with the technology we have from the vocabulary which used to be called modern architecture'.[41] This is how nineteenth-century architecture

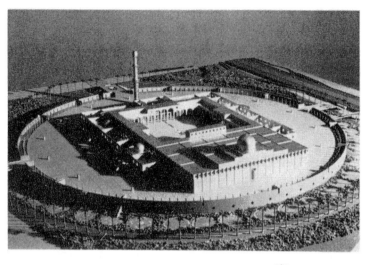

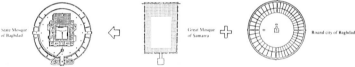

34. Baghdad State Mosque Competition, Minoru Takeyama, 1983. The above diagram (round city + Samarra Mosque = State Mosque) was in Takeyama's submission.

was created, as Bofill and Venturi are aware, and for that very reason everything about that century was abhorred by the early moderns. In his remarkable housing project, Les Echelles du Baroque in Paris, Bofill has demonstrated that when he rummages about in Western history, he knows how to make poetry of a new kind. But the same unfortunately cannot be said about the outcome of the few weeks he must have spent rummaging about in the world of Islamic architecture. The result is ponderous and funereal pastiche.

The Venturi solution to the brief is more interesting. Stressing its 'unequivocally egalitarian' expression in the service of monumentality, the architectural trick lay in floating a *Fantasia*-like dome over the courtyard, the normally open-air *sahan*, instead of over the prayer hall

61

which it traditionally covers (Figs. 35, 36, 37). The interior is treated like something out of Disneyland crossed with the scenery from Errol Flynn's film, *The Thief of Baghdad*. The form of the dome is generated by making a gigantic Claes Oldenburg-style enlargement (Fig. 38) of the *muqarnass* (typically a small-scale Islamic decorative device for making the transition from square to circle). Now the 'dome reveals itself as a tree within a courtyard, a huge tree, but light and airy, whose great uplifted canopy shades the *sahan* and the people beneath'.[42] Secularizing the dome in the name of 'the people' by placing it over the *sahan* instead of the holy sanctuary of the prayer hall, meant that it could be bigger, more monumental (the *sahan* is always much larger than the prayer hall). Yet this overwhelming form originates in a tiny traditional piece of decoration (the *muqarnass*). Thus, equality and monumentality, a theoretically perfect combination, have acquired a new architectural expression.

Looked at the other way around, however, the architecture can also be taken as a celebration of the fact that although the people are not free in Iraq, at least they are all equal in the degree of their monumental unfreedom. This is, after all, how the Ba'th understand their socialism (freedom is economic or social, never political). Their equality is the equality of complete homogeneity, absolute suppression of personality, where everyone is equally unfree before His authority. What happened to being 'separate' in the darkness of a restaurant or in the alcoves of a Las Vegas casino, those ostensibly great substitutes for 'big-scale, unified' traditional monumentality rejected by Venturi in 1972? For that matter, what happened to the 'traditional monumentality' which was supposed to have been replaced by the casino? It seems to have sneaked in again through the back door. He got one thing right, however: his mosque, like the casino, would be filled with 'crowds of anonymous individuals without explicit connection with each other'.

Is Venturi playing post-modern games and having fun with tradition? — a perfectly reasonable thing to do, however unsuited for this auspicious occasion. Maybe he was deploying irony and wit to deal with the contradictory circumstances in which he found himself in Baghdad. But what is the point of a joke when neither your client nor any potential user of your monument has any idea of the ground rules that are supposed to make something funny? By definition

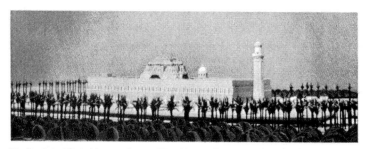

35. Baghdad State Mosque Competition, Venturi, Rauch and Scott Brown, 1983. View of model.

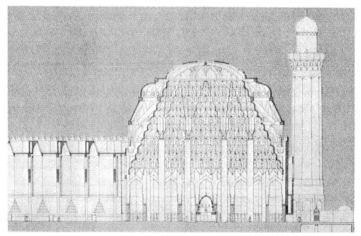

36. Section through dome

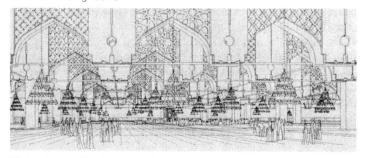

37. Interior view of main prayer hall

post-modern architecture is about forms that ordinary people find easy to relate to. At least architects like Mies van der Rohe and Frank Lloyd Wright would not have given a damn, expecting from the start to be understood only by other elites. Nor are we able to construe Venturi's scheme as a brilliant post-modern spoof on Post-Modernism, because by now the architecture is taking itself with the same deadly seriousness as the Modernism it replaced.

When a Pop architect ends up celebrating a tyranny in the name of equality and in the style of Disneyland, a very strange cultural dialectic of space and time is created; at least as strange as the one created in this essay. But oppositions, however hybrid, illuminate both sides: the West versus the East; regional identity versus 'international style'; commercialism versus art; Dadaism versus the art establishment. The problem is that even in a godless, anti-utopian, post-modern world, radical eclecticism and wit are not enough to create meaning. Monuments still have to refer to something other than themselves. The Romans had their empire and organization. The medieval world had its theology. The Enlightenment had its metaphysics of Reason and Progress. The early moderns had their machine and technology aesthetic. The Nazis had their racial rhetoric. And even Saddam Husain has his party values. Does Venturi want a share in them?

In an astute observation the critic Charles Jencks noted that one of the 'defining characteristics of Post-Modernism is its pursuit of odd metaphysics, "after strange gods" as it were'. Like the Surrealist painter, the post-modern architect 'crystallizes his own spiritual realm around the possible metaphors at hand. The metaphysics are then expressed as either implicit or explicit metaphor which is signified in the form.'[43] But Pop architecture can be anti-Pop; Venturi's cleverness is thrown wildly off target by the sobering facts of Baghdad. Wherein lies the significance of his 'inverted' conventional cliché on this grand Ba'thist occasion? In the transformation of the *muqarnass* into a huge dome? When an architect has nothing more substantial than cleverness around which to wrap his metaphors, they take revenge and slap him in the face. Whether we like it or not, we are dealing here with momentous issues of life and death, barbarism versus civilization. This focus, one might even say, Saddam Husain understands better than Venturi.

Art is subordinate to meaning; it cannot float aimlessly in a sea of

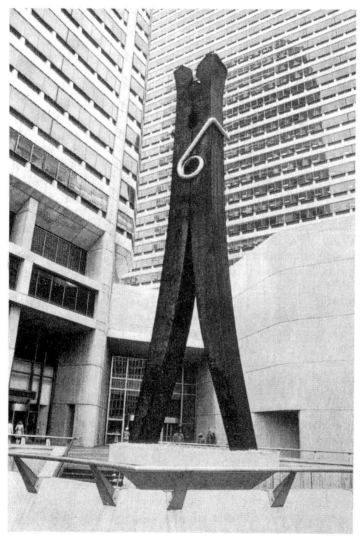

38. 'Clothespin'. Height 13.5 metres. Philadelphia, Claes Oldenburg, 1976. Like the hot-dog stand (Fig. 32) but from the vantage-point of 'fine art' (not crass commercialism), Oldenburg's 'Clothespin' is a perfect equivalent of Saddam Husain's monument.

65

contradiction, variety, acquiescence and 'acategorical thought' without paying a price. With Andy Warhol that price turned out to be the death of art. By 1983, Venturi had journeyed from acceptance to glorification to ideologization of vulgarity. Fortunately for him, he did not win the competition. No one did. On the last day of the widely publicized adjudication jamboree, the President stalked out of the hall in a dramatic scene reminiscent of the start of the Iraq–Iran war.[44] When the results were later announced, it turned out that none of the schemes were good enough and it was the President's wish that six competitors, including Venturi and Bofill, get together to produce a joint scheme under his guidance. Venturi refused, and reportedly left Baghdad furious. (But he, along with the other participants, were commissioned for other projects as part of that city's massive urban renewal programme, and therefore helped shape its 'new face'.[45])

What would have happened had Venturi's mosque been built in the city of Saddam Husain's monument? Despite its scale and intelligence, it would have been sucked empty of the meanings the architect had in mind, only to be filled up again with an affirmation whose spirit derives from the monument. So in the end which is the greater work, and why?

In place of art, ugliness – which Venturi wanted to extol – has acquired a meaning that he never intended. Thus although the vulgarity of Saddam Husain's monument takes it out of the realm of art, in the end by playing this game, the President defeats art. But this was the whole point of 'Pop' art and architecture. Where are we to go from here?

From around the middle of the 1970s, vulgarity in the West was discovered by more and more people to have aesthetic value. A wholesale retreat from the values of the Modern Movement and the so-called 'International Style' in architecture had ensued. Today kitsch objects, or 'junk art', and hitherto rejected historical paraphernalia of every sort (Doric columns, pediments and other classical bits and pieces) are being appropriated and deployed by artists and architects everywhere, just as 'primitive art' or an 'architecture without architects' was appropriated by a previous generation.[46] Classicism, Post-Modernism and nineteenth-century eclecticism are the dominant modes of expression among some of the most enterprising architects practising today. Invariably the assault on modernism is cloaked in populism disguised as an attack on the 'elitist codes' of the early pioneers (who, incidentally, attacked their forerunners of the nineteenth century in similar ways).[47]

Beginning with the visual appropriation of kitsch to Post-Modernism, and nowadays Deconstructionism, in architecture, sculpture and painting, *a new visual language* is taking shape incorporating themes of irony, contradiction, ambiguity, eclecticism, new notions of beauty as dissonance not harmony, along with historicism and a consciously schizophrenic stance towards the past.[48] Everywhere, it seems, the language of visual formalism in the plastic arts — where the values of line, colour, mass, surface, volume, texture and space ruled from Bauhaus days — is being neglected in favour of values that have always ruled in the written arts (literature and poetry). The monumental constructions of Claes Oldenburg and Hans Hollein are a case in point. Such artists don't even want to invent new forms but rest their art on spectacular transformations in our perception of the scale of common objects: floppy toilets, hard apples, a packet of matches as big as a Manhattan skyscraper, a building in the shape of a spark plug, a monument in the shape of a clothespin. Even the traditional materials on which the whole training of an artist used to be based, are being done away with. I see no evidence that these new values in art are any more popular than the old ones of the Bauhaus, the Modern Movement or the Beaux-Arts schools. Nonetheless, this new language of the arts has irreversibly revolutionized our notions of vulgarity, of 'what is a monument', and 'what is sculpture or architecture'. To what ultimate end is a matter of speculation.

Precisely because of this same transformation in our sensibilities wrought in the 1960s by artists like Andy Warhol and architects like Robert Venturi (among others, of course), we can set aside considerations of the art of Saddam Husain's monument, and instead begin to appreciate it as an extraordinary piece of Iraqi kitsch.

Kitsch is something other than simply a work in poor taste. There is a kitsch attitude. Kitsch behavior. The kitsch-man's need for kitsch: it is the need to gaze into the mirror of the beautifying lie and to be moved to tears of gratification at one's own reflection.

Milan Kundera[49]

7
The Kitsch
of Baghdad

'Kitschness' is an unselfconscious attitude, an unreflective norm of behaviour necessarily shared by large numbers of people. The moment we call something 'kitsch', we enter the exclusive company of snobs and artists. The very idea of kitsch or 'junk art' (like junk food) implies the simultaneity of two sets of values: the values of junk which we all take for granted (whenever we step inside a McDonald's restaurant), and the always 'elitist' values of art (haute cuisine and health food shops). The 'kitschness' of an object erodes in proportion with the number of people who selfconsciously view it as such. Thus, for instance, if the appreciation of the Pop architecture of Los Angeles by way of Post-Modernism goes much further, Americans may find themselves slapping conservation orders on such buildings as the previously mentioned hot dog stand (see Fig. 32) in a way that the English are permanently fond of doing with the whole of their architectural inheritance. The architectural profession used to consider Doric columns and casino interiors as quintessential kitsch, until Venturi adopted the latter and Bofill the former. We may hate a piece of kitsch, or we may find it endearing, but it is never either ugly or beautiful from the standpoint of art. Beauty in the strictly artistic sense has to be *created* by the transformative powers of a human agent, always standing alone outside the crowd. By contrast kitsch is just there, like the fast food chain around the corner, or like William Blake's 'nature' in the nineteenth century (itself, by the way, a romantic construct which is no more natural than any other human artefact).

The irony is that human beings can no more do away with kitsch than they can do away with art. Kitsch is like the words of our speech which we normally pass over quickly without withdrawing from circulation to contemplate their meanings. To do so would destroy the possibility of communication, action and ultimately even thought itself. We understand each other, and ourselves, as Paul Valéry so nicely put it, 'only thanks to our rapid passage over words'.[50]

But the words of speech have many properties which separate them out from one another even though our need for all of them is the same. Thinking is not mere speech; it is pondering over words, their properties and meanings, just as art is about 'stopping' images and everyday objects in order to fashion them anew. A 'still-life', a landscape, the human figure, William Blake's flower and grain of sand, even Saddam Husain's monument, are potentially all as enigmatical as a word like 'love' which we use all the time. As Kundera has defined it, kitsch, like love, is rooted exclusively in the human capacity for sentiment, as opposed to reason, abstraction or description. Unlike love, however, there is something false or misdirected about the sentiment; but not insincere, as Quentin Bell maintained regarding 'bad' art.

So defined, kitsch is today rampant in the Arab world with regard to what everyone likes to think of as their *turath* (heritage). *Turath* as kitsch is a fixation on a 'collective' self in the same way that the President's monument betrays a psychological fixation with his own power. To illustrate: During an important symposium and exhibition on modern Arab art held in Casablanca, the Iraqi painter Nazar Salim put forward the idea that the cultural project of Arab artists was 'arabizing art'. The Tunisian artist and critic, Nasir bin al-Shaykh, objected on the grounds that the real problem was not how to arabize art, but how to arabize the artist himself so that he was able to reject all Western influences and paint or write about art inspired only by his own visual heritage and what Muslim ancients had to say about it. The very idea of 'individual expression', he went on to say, was Western in origin and ought to be replaced by collective art.[51]

But in no Arab country is the fixation with *turath* more evident than in Iraq, where official patronage in the last decade has resulted in record sums being spent on promoting it in culture and the arts. *Turath* is first praised and then propagandized in the spirit of the beautifying lie in endless conferences, the activities of Iraqi Cultural Centres across the world, travelling exhibitions of Iraqi art and folklore, international art exhibitions, and fully-financed literary and poetry festivals regularly held in Baghdad and attended by the biggest names in Arabic letters.[52] The impressive art journal *UR*, dedicated to the *turath* of Iraq, was financed by the Iraqi Cultural Centre in London to the highest standards and with the participation of the most accomplished writers, critics and artists. Everyone who is anyone in the arts was involved, and not only for perfectly understandable pecuniary reasons. They were involved because however harsh the regime, all identify with the idea that creative expression and *turath* march hand in hand against the twin evils of slavish adherence to the past and imitative Westernism, as Saddam Husain so nicely put it during a one-week conference on 'Our Architectural Heritage and the New Arab Architecture' held in Baghdad in the same week he launched the Iraq—Iran war.[53]

The problem with 'inventing *turath*' is that there is actually no continuity with a historic past. When the Ba'th finally came around to realizing a twenty-year-old dream to rebuild Babylon (a committee of Iraqi archaeologists and architects had succeeded in scotching the idea in 1969), they built the five-thousand-year-old capital of Nebuchadnezzar out of thermalite blocks 'in the style of the Barbican', according to one English observer.

Rising from the ransacked jumble of ruins by the Al-Hilla river is a
new tower of Babel, together with crenellated royal apartments built
with what look like ochre Lego bricks...
    About a third of the site still awaits the builders' trowels. Great
blocks of original Babylonian masonry are heaped haphazardly on
dusty and crumbling foundations. Here, it is still possible to sit and
ponder ancient history in silence. The Iraqis prefer to admire the new
version.[54]

Every Friday, people drive out from Baghdad in droves to visit
Nebuchadnezzar's new palace. 'It's prettier than where we live,' said
one teenage student amidst a group of her friends.[55] Although the
Ishtar Gate, which once stood on Processional Way, ancient Babylon's
main thoroughfare, is only half the size of the original and its
crenellated parapet detailing is based on guesswork, the new gate is
still very big and it is clad in bright blue tiles decorated with dragons
and bulls (Fig. 39). The gate opens on to courtyards and five hundred
rooms which took one thousand Sudanese labourers three years of
work, seven days a week. An image of Babylon which many people
can identify with has finally been created in place of the piles of mud,
foundation traces and stone blocks which was all that was left of the
real thing (see Fig. 40). Nebuchadnezzar had left instruction in
cuneiform script on tablets of clay, which, it seems, are finally being
carried out. He urged his successors to repair his royal edifices, which
for identification purposes had bricks inserted in the walls, with an
inscription announcing that they were the work of 'Nebuchadnezzar,
King of Babylon from far sea to far sea'. New Babylon's walls are
similarly being earmarked for history with bricks inserted on which is
inscribed: 'Rebuilt in the era of the leader Saddam Husain.'
    'The invention of tradition', as Eric Hobsbawm has pointed out,
goes on all the time and in every society.[56] However, it tends to
become creatively exuberant during periods of rapid change. The faster
'old' Baghdad disappeared, the more urgent became the desire to
fantasize about how wonderful it always was. In the early 1980s,
Amanat al-Asima drew up conservation plans for the Kadhimiyya and
al-Gailani districts which proposed sticking all vehicular circulation
and parking underground, in a vast concrete rabbit warren of roads
and parking lots. Pedestrians then pop out to live in picturesque
courtyard houses. All this for the sake of 'keeping alive Baghdadi

71

housing traditions, but with the introduction of the latest technology such as solar panels for air conditioning'.[57] As in Babylon, 'conservation', we discover, entails rebuilding new courtyard houses in somebody's image of a nonexistent old. Experience shows that 'the people' do not choose to live in such housing, but even they don't find anything wrong with the idea. In Ba'thi Iraq not only politics, but history, sociology, literature, the imagination, everything is subservient to the sweet lie.

The role of a successful new monument in such a city is to transfix the fantasy so that it enters into the service of some new need. In Ismail Fattah's monument (see Fig. 15), for instance, the symbolic vocabulary of the ceramic clad dome, stripped of all association with building, was pushed beyond its traditional religious association to commemorate a new secular idea (martyrdom for the sake of the Arab nation or the Ba'thi state, with the souls of the dead rising between the two halves[58]). And the once hated regime of the Hashemites, so bloodily overthrown in 1958, is rehabilitated by replicating the statue of King Faisal I riding a horse which was torn down by the mob in 1958 (see Fig. 71). The copy is located at the entrance to Saddam Husain's new Haifa street. While the plethora of civic monuments in 1980s Baghdad certainly reshaped the physical fabric of the city, their principal function is to forge this new collective identity supposedly handed down by history, but in fact motivated by a Ba'thi-led modernization that is a radical rupture with history, greater than anything experienced by Iraqis since the break-up of the Ottoman empire. And Iraqis collaborate in the venture, partly because they have no alternative, and partly because they experience the anguish of wanting to become a real collective (a modern nation), while not being one.

In the name of glorifying Baghdad and the traditions of Mesopotamia the Iraqi sculptor, Mohammed Ghani, has made realistic sculptures of: Aladdin's genie emerging from the lamp, Shahrazade and Shahryar (Fig. 41), Sindbad the sailor anchored to a raft in the middle of the Tigris, the poet Al-Mutannabi (no one has any idea what he might have looked like), a six-metre high imaginative reconstruction of Abu Ja'far al-Mansur (the first Abbasid Caliph) in stone, Hammurabi in bronze, and the mythical figure of Gilgamesh next to a much larger sculpture of Saddam Husain. Before becoming

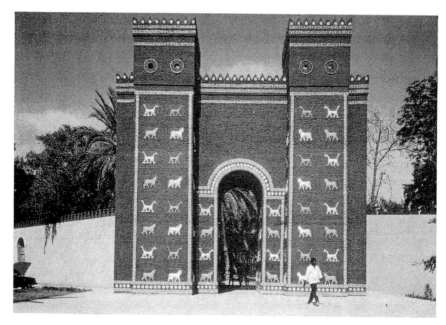

39. The Ishtar Gate at half-size, based largely on guesswork.

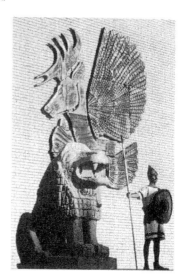

40. A guard standing to attention at the Palace of Nebuchadnezzar. An Iraqi equivalent of the changing of the guards at Buckingham Palace?

73

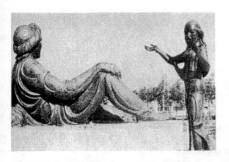

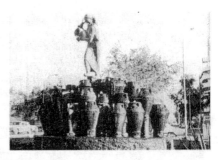

41. 'Shahrazad and Shahryar' (from the *Arabian Nights*) on Abu Nuwas street. Bronze, 4.25 metres, 1975. Mohammed Ghani.

42. Morgiana pouring boiling oil into forty vats to kill off the thieves hiding inside. Otherwise known as the Fountain of Kuhrumaneh on Sa'adoon street, Baghdad. Bronze, 3.30 metres, 1971. Mohammed Ghani.

involved with the Victory Arch he made a bronze edifice in a busy traffic intersection on Sa'adoon street depicting Morgiana the slave girl in a scene from "Ali Baba and the Forty Thieves' (Fig. 42). The original executing artist for the arch was Khalid al-Rahal. His monument to the Unknown Soldier is, of course, quintessential kitsch on a grand scale (see Fig. 17). Both Rahal and Ghani are counted among the best Iraqi sculptors of the twentieth century.[59]

Baghdad became littered with such kitsch in the 1980s, both in the form of public monuments and most prominently in buildings like those strung along Haifa street and elsewhere (Figs. 14, 44, 45). Decorated pastiche façades papered over conventional concrete boxes (in the name of Post-Modernism?) − it is hard to imagine how anyone could so successfully combine the worst in everything. The spirit of Saddam Husain's monument is in them all, if not the degree of his vulgarity.

Here is history, literature and a people's myths and legends become kitsch; it is revivalism of a sort that is neither creative nor rooted in a deep feeling for what is being revived. The irony is that even a scholarly copy (where there are models to copy from) has more integrity to it than such a relentless outpouring of nostalgia. The British architect Quinlan Terry, for example, designs new buildings which look as if they have come straight out of a Georgian, Edwardian and Palladian time warp (Fig. 46). To do this he has to rediscover

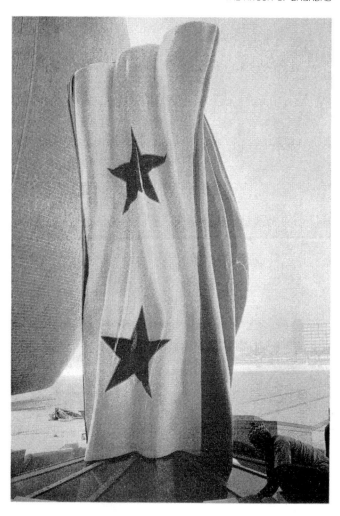

43. A metal Iraqi flag/sculpture 5 metres high located at the centre of the *Shaheed* Monument (Fig. 15), the nation's symbol fluttering nobly in the breeze: an instant frozen in time and space. The intention was the reverse of the ponderous effect achieved. The flag/sculpture protrudes through a glass skylight and its base projects down into an underground museum from which it appears to be floating in space. The effect looking up from the cavernous interior is surreal.

75

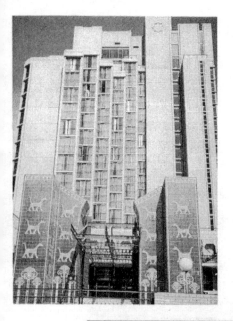

44. Babylon Hotel, Baghdad. The entrance is a miniaturized replica of what the architect imagines the real Ishtar Gate might have looked like three thousand years ago (compare with Fig. 39).

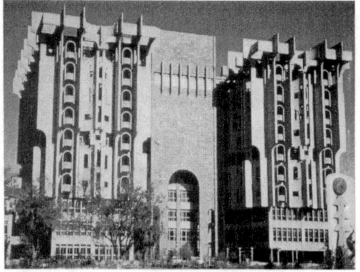

45. Ministry of Industry Building, Baghdad

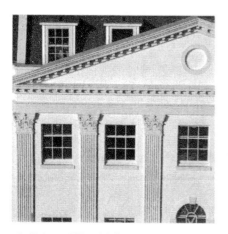

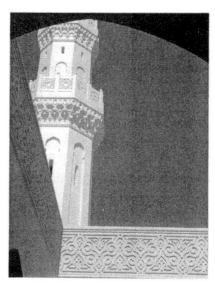

46. Richmond Riverside Development, London. Quinlan Terry, 1988.

47. Minaret detail from Suleyman Mosque, Jedda. Abdel Wahed Wakil, 1980.

classical detailing; he has to *become* a classical architect all over again. However pointless, such a project is no longer easy to do well and requires a big imaginative leap away from our modern heritage. The ideas of Hasan Fathy on the mud brick architecture of Upper Egypt, and the work of his former student, Abdel Wahed el-Wakil, are similar examples from the Arab world (Fig. 47). They have integrity as objects and command respect, even though their widespread application defies common sense as well as modern planning, building and technological criteria. By contrast the buildings along Haifa street are window-dressing exercises, just as the new civic monuments of Baghdad are pure pastiche under the cover of reviving Mesopotamian and Islamic traditions. Mohammed Ghani provided the justification that they all loudly claim for themselves when he said:

> I have discovered that Western imitation is a dead end road ... whereas benefiting from the inheritance gives the smell [*sic*!] of seriousness without discontinuity; it provides subjective identity and independence for the artist in his subject matter and in his technique.[60]

77

Where do Baghdadis stand in relation to the artist? ... Will
they find him on Rashid street? In the public gardens? ...
Take the houses: the first thing you notice as you enter is the
furniture, expensive and compacted in everywhere. Taste is
not important ... The furniture is comfortable and the latest
model from Beirut. (Oh, how beautiful!) Then you turn your
eyes and find pocket romances and the Monday magazine
instead of books ... You raise your eyes to the walls, what
do you see? If they are not bare then they are decorated with
a big picture of the grandfather, and an even bigger one of the
head of the household in his youth ... When the taste is
more elevated, and the head of the household starts to feel the
need for 'art', then you will find a calendar for the Cadillac
company decorated with a pretty girl ... This is the public's
taste ...

A well-meaning poet has said of us that we are enemies of
the people. He has said that we ought to be fought by every
patriotic Iraqi. We are enemies it seems because the food of
the people is pocket romances, the Monday magazine,
Egyptian films, and nightclubs. This well-meaning poet
obviously does not understand [art].

Jewad Salim,
Public lecture, 1951[61]

8
Turath
as Art

Before there was *turath*-as-kitsch, there was *turath*-as-art. In Iraq, the
heritage of ancient Mesopotamia and Islamic civilization became the
source of a rich artistic expression long before the Ba'thi regime.
Visually this first blossomed in the work of Jewad Salim, Iraq's most
gifted and influential modern artist. But its development, refinement
and self-definition, whether by direct extension or through opposition,
owes a great deal to other pioneers of Iraqi art: painters like Shakir
Hasan aal Sa'id, Faik Hasan, Lorna Salim, Hafidh al-Duroobi, Jamil
Hamoodi, Mahmood Sabri, Ismail al-Shaikhly; sculptors like the early
Khalid al-Rahal and Mohammed Ghani; critics like Jabra Ibrahim
Jabra; architects like Mohammed Makiya and Rifa'at Chadirchi. These

are the artists who forged the first modern, peculiarly Iraqi, visual tradition in the arts between the 1940s and the 1960s, a tradition which in the approving words of Shakir Hasan so succeeded in cultivating a 'collective vision' among Iraqi artists, that by the 1970s 'everyone' was working 'in the name of modernity as *turath*'.[62]

The first creators of this tradition, unlike their later followers, had sipped long and deep from the waters of Europe before returning to work in Iraq in the 1940s. Largely through their efforts, Baghdad became in the 1950s the centre of some of the most dynamic and original experimentation in the visual arts anywhere in the Arab world. Certainly in no other Arab country did visual talent cohere into such a powerful, self-reinforcing, particular way of looking at felt reality, rooted in Iraqi experience. An indisputably *Iraqi* way of thinking about the plastic arts came into being, made up of talented, opinionated and generally very productive individuals knocking against each other, yet springing out in different directions. And in no other Arab country did an individual of the towering talent of Jewad Salim emerge.

The influence of the Iraqi school can still be seen in the work of painters from the Arab Gulf countries who studied in the Baghdad School of Fine Arts. It is also noticeable for its absence in a country like the Lebanon, the main other Arab country where considerable visual talent emerged, acutely conscious of what was going on in Western art circles. However, Lebanese artists remained uninfluenced by each other, uninterested in the history or traditions of their country, and generally contented with developing individual styles centred on portraiture, still-life and nature. The outcome has been that it 'is difficult to identify a Lebanese tradition or even to trace a "period" or "movement" fostered at the time by like-minded artists'.[63]

The opposite was the case in Iraq. Instead of nature or still-life, Iraqi reference points were various art forms like Assyrian and Sumerian sculpture, the scenes of Baghdadi life drawn by the thirteenth-century artist Yahya al-Wasiti, arabesque geometry, Islamic calligraphy, applied art and architecture (particularly of the Abbasid period), and themes from daily life, folk culture and rural society. The dynamic tension between painters like Jewad Salim and Faik Hasan in the early years, between architects like Rifa'at Chadirchi and Mohammed Makiya, between the 'Primitives' of the 1940s, the 'Pioneers' and the

'Baghdad Group' of the 1950s, is proverbial in Iraqi art circles. Later all this original and creative diversity was going to be too neatly subsumed under the rubric of a 'search for the features of the national personality in art'.[64] Continuity with a broken past and ancient glories, or a 'revolutionary' transcendence of the historical gap and a parallel preoccupation with tragedy, heroic folklore, and 'struggling through art' against misery and oppression, increasingly became the dominant motifs of Iraqi visual culture.[65]

Before everyone jumped on to the bandwagon of *turath*, artists like Jewad Salim were acutely conscious of addressing only a tiny circle of people in the new 'elitist' language of modern art. In his 1951 public lecture, Salim spoke critically, ironically, even bitterly of the standards of public taste in Iraq. Yet barely two decades later and the name Jewad Salim had turned into a myth among literate Iraqis; the same poets who had called him an 'enemy of the people' in the early 1950s, began to recite odes in his praise. Today public art flourishes and artists are fêted inside Iraq as they have not been since the time of the Caliphs.

Shakir Hasan attributes this withering away of 'the gulf between the masses and the artist in Iraq' to the success of Salim's project of appropriating *turath*. He writes that after the 1958 revolution, 'the artist was able to put his trust in the state', and a new period in Iraqi art opened, a period in which it was no longer the artist's responsibility to 'safeguard' the public taste, even though that same public used to think that what was being safeguarded in its name was 'from another world' – to paraphrase Jewad Salim's opening words in 1951. By the 1960s, the state was preparing to espouse *turath*, and all the artist had to do, Shakir Hasan reasons, was forge ahead busily absorbing *turath* and folklore in the knowledge that he had been freed from the historical responsibility which an artist like Jewad Salim had previously had to shoulder along with a small circle of like-minded people.[66]

A considerable, specifically Iraqi achievement in the visual domain coincided with backwardness in matters of thought generally and mediocrity in the literary arts (with notable exceptions like that of the poet Badr Shakir al-Sayab). Here Beirut, Cairo and Damascus were pre-eminent. Even the celebrated 'father' of Arab nationalism in modern Arab politics, Satia' al-Husri, who established the Baghdad

Museum of Antiquities and Institute of Fine Arts in the 1930s, was a Syrian. It was Husri who first brought the young Jewad Salim and other budding artists to work in the museum restoring old reliefs, and later to teach painting and sculpture in the new institute.[67] And it was Husri who first encouraged these young men to look to the traditions of their native land until his forced exile in 1941. 'The great educator', as he was known in Iraq, was replaced by men like Sami Shawkat who in his capacity as director general of education circulated a proto-fascist speech entitled 'The Manufacture of Death' throughout all public schools. Shawkat not Husri was the precursor of a new virulent strand of pan-Arabism which eventually crystallized into the politics of the Iraqi Ba'th.[68]

Saddam Husain's monument has therefore a cultural ancestry; it is the bizarre offspring of a marriage enacted at the outer limits of a considerable artistic achievement and numbing intellectual primitivism. *Turath* as art and *turath* as kitsch are indissolubly linked in modern Iraq. I shall examine *turath* as the wellspring of the Iraqi school of thinking about art through the prism of its most famous artefact: Jewad Salim's 1961 monument to freedom, widely recognized to be his *magnum opus*, and probably the most important work of public art ever commissioned from a modern Arab artist. Certainly, until Saddam Husain and his monuments came along in the 1980s, it was the biggest work to be commissioned in the land that had first invented the idea of a monument, for the last two and a half thousand years.

The 1961 Freedom Monument

Until 1958, Baghdad boasted a total of three public sculptures all built by non-Iraqi artists after the collapse of Ottoman rule in 1918: General Maude, the British officer who took Iraq from the Ottomans in 1914, cast in bronze outside the British embassy; King Faisal, founder of the modern Iraqi state, near the radio and television broadcasting station; and the innocuous figure of Muhsin Saadoon, a former Iraqi prime minister. Only General Maude and King Faisal were depicted on horseback (symbol of a higher authority), which, along with their strategic locations, had something to do with what happened on the morning of 14 July 1958. Angry and enthusiatic crowds gathered around General Maude and King Faisal and with ropes, straining hands and ever so willing hearts they pulled their edifices down to the ground, smashed them up, and cast the fragments into the Tigris. Thus ended the monarchy and Western influence inside Iraq (see Fig. 71).

The scene left a deep impression on Salim who was commissioned in 1959 by the fledgling republic to celebrate the revolution in a new monumental sculpture. He expended extraordinary efforts on it under difficult conditions, successfully resisting the attempt of the President, Brigadier 'Abdul Karim Qassem, to have his image included. *Nasb al-Hurriyya*, as the monument is known in Arabic (Fig. 48), still presides over the heart of Baghdad at the end of a public garden facing Liberation square and Jumhourriyya bridge, having survived at least one attempt (in the second half of the 1960s) to pull it down on a count of paganism. The devoutly Muslim President 'Aref, acting on the Muslim injunction against figurative representation, backed down under public pressure. By contrast *nasb al-Hurriyya* survived Saddam Husain's reign only because the Arab Ba'th Socialist Party holds that its notion of freedom is the legitimate heir and logical culmination of what was begun in 1958, even though the public long ago ceased to be a force in civic affairs.[69]

Public art on a comparable scale would not be attempted again until Saddam Husain began reshaping Baghdad in the 1980s. The 1961 monument to freedom, which replaced those of General Maude and King Faisal, is therefore a kind of bridge between the Baghdad of the 1940s where a remarkable artist achieved artistic maturity, and the Baghdad of the 1980s which gave birth to Saddam Husain's Victory Arch. It is a monument that belongs to the revolutionary city of the late 1950s and 1960s. For finally there is not one city of Baghdad, but three different cities, to each one of which there corresponds a monument: a form in whose physical attributes the gods of that city acquire presence.

Jewad Salim felt that his monument had to signify the dawn of a new world as intensely as the masses on that fateful July morning had torn down the old. He also knew that because this was a commission with a definite subject, it had to end up as a compromise. His task was to serve the outside purpose, celebrate an event, yet preserve in the object the integrity of a work of art imbued with a larger universality

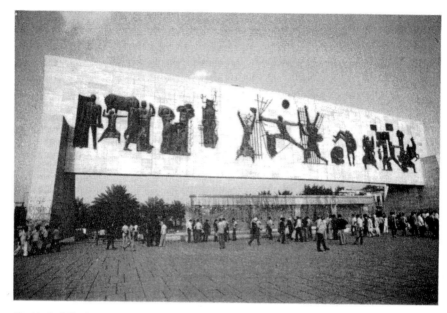

48. *Nasb al-Hurriyya* (the Freedom Monument), bronze on travertine. Slab dimensions: 50 metres x 10 metres. Slab lifted 6 metres off the ground. Jewad Salim, 1961.

of meaning. Jewad Salim did not live to see his meanings metamorphose into such objects as Saddam Husain's monument. He would have been horrified. In January 1961, at forty-one years of age, he died of a heart attack brought on by stress and overwork during the final stages of construction.

Nasb al-Hurriyya is a visual narrative of the 1958 revolution told through symbols which the artist had been developing in the whole body of his work. Strikingly modern, yet clearly paying homage to its sources in Assyrian and Babylonian wall-relief traditions, the monument is organized as fourteen separate bronze castings averaging eight metres in height. These are meant to be 'read' like a verse of Arabic poetry, from right to left, from the events leading up to the revolution, to the revolution itself and an ensuing harmony.

In the beginning (far right, reading as in Arabic script from right to left) 'there was a horse', the artist is telling us (Arab symbol for purity

83

of origin, good breeding, masculinity and strength). The horse, unlike its placid bronze counterparts of pre-1958 Iraq, is teeming with vitality, rearing up on its hind legs having thrown its rider. Agitated men strain around him (the masses? – Fig. 49).[70] The motion is chaotic, violent and directed leftwards by force of the horse's arching neck. Maintaining all its vigour, however, it becomes orderly, exuding determination in the figure striding forward, modern placards and banners raised high. Innocence and hope show the way, leaping off the marble background towards us in the shape of a child, the only completely three-dimensional figure of the relief (Fig. 50). Man is accompanied by woman, just as purposeful but with a face wrought by emotion (wailing, angry?).

This first sequence ends with motherhood weeping over the martyred son. Iraqi history is often portrayed as the playing out of a great tragedy with martyrdom as its major theme, particularly since the death of Husain, the son of 'Ali, on the plains of Kerbala in 680 A D. Motherhood follows, encircling new life with love and affection (see the variety and intensity of facial expression, achieved with extraordinary economy of form). Revolutions may have their victims but they also always have their new generations (Fig. 51).

The centrepiece of the relief is made of three castings. On the right is the political prisoner (Fig. 52) whose iron cage is shown caving in under the pressure of a man whose back is violently lacerated (the victimized masses?). But the bent bars are only torn asunder through the taut spring-like tension of the soldier in the middle: the artist's concession to the role of the army in 1958 (the centrepiece was the only part of the monument shown in advance to the regime for its approval). Finally to the left of the centre section, freedom in the ancient Greek symbol of a torch-bearing woman surges out into the daylight looking towards its liberator (see Fig. 70). Asked why freedom had no feet, Salim is reported to have said: 'Feet stick to the ground; I wanted her to soar high.'[71]

Calm follows all this turbulence. The restless motion, anger, tension and pain of the revolution ceases. Peace descends. Repose enters the people's hearts. Iron bars turn into branches; and eyes close with serenity because peace is an offering which knows no fear. The Tigris (which in Arabic means palm trees) and the Euphrates (fertility) are represented by two women, the one carrying palm fronds and the

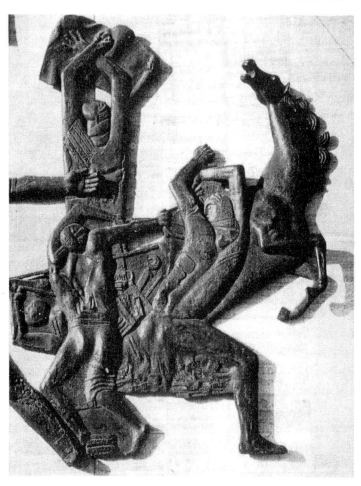

49. The horse

other pregnant. Two male peasants (symbolizing the Arabs and the Kurds but in the dress of a Sumerian and an Assyrian) look towards their female counterparts (the Tigris and the Euphrates) holding a single spade between them, to represent the one country they share, and brimming with self-confidence. In production through agriculture,

85

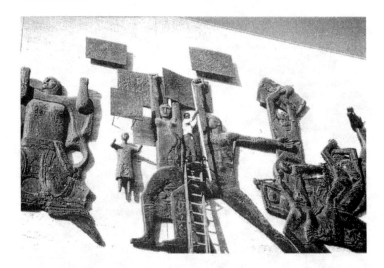

50. The first half of the story

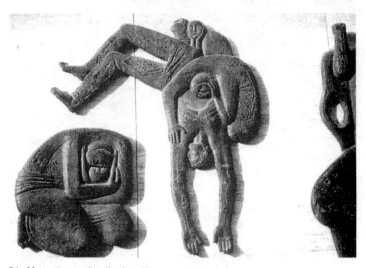

51. Martyrdom and motherhood

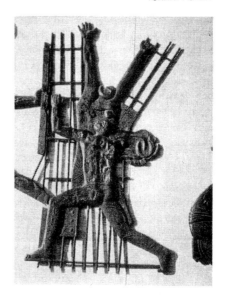

52. Releasing the political prisoner. The influence of Picasso, in particular his masterpiece 'Guernica', is openly acknowledged in this detail.

animal wealth (signified by the ox, an ancient Iraqi symbol) and industry (the self-confident worker on the far left), the story of freedom as it was understood by millions of Iraqis in those hope-filled years comes to a happy end.

We know that something went wrong with this image of freedom. Freedom, is turned out, had no foothold in Iraq. But as a criticism of the monument, this misses the point entirely. Art has no predictive value. Nor is it easily harnessed to a message. Considered separately, the weakest part of the monument is the centre section because the eclectic symbolism of the three castings which comprise it reinforces the tendency to organize its meaning in simple-minded ways, such as those used by al-Bayati, the chairman of the committee for the monument.[72] But where does quality lie in an object like the Freedom Monument, If not in its imagery? Not only Bayati, but also the most sophisticated Iraqi critics and artists (Jabra and Shakir Hasan, for instance) continuously confuse the themes and sheer size of the 1961 monument with its worth as a work of art, something Jewad Salim himself would not have done. The fact is, something purely 'artistic' and far more mundane than imagery went wrong with this artefact.

87

Jewad Salim was a maker and composer of strikingly Iraqi symbols, not a storyteller. He knew how to break down a form to its bare essentials, 'analyse' it with an economy of line and concentrated expressiveness that is breathtaking. From the same formal point of view, however, his modern wall-relief, unlike its Assyrian and Babylonian precursors, is not woven into its city context; nor does it create its own uniquely visual imaginary space within which the exquisitely sculptured elements could take on their intended relational meaning. The great travertine-clad slab in *nasb al-Hurriyya*, fifty metres long and ten metres high, is supposed to have been inspired by the monumental gates of Assyria and Babylon. But it strikes me as having more in common with the sweeping modern concrete forms of Oscar Niemeyer (unless of course one thinks of every post and lintel construction as Mesopotamian in origin). In any case the height of the slab, elevated as it is six metres off the ground, utterly destroys the *Gestalt* of the monument, and removes the viewer from any proximity to the detail of the art. This was not the artist's original intention. Salim wanted the work to be a 'wall' at ground level, but the architect for the project, Rifa'at Chadirchi, insisted on raising the figures to achieve a more 'monumental' effect. The result is that the monument faces a public, not of people, but of cars in traffic jams (observe in Fig. 48 the indifference of passers-by to the monument, which faces Tahrir square rather than the garden at its back).

A visual work of art is a self-sustained unity of form within which all parts receive artistic meaning only by their relation to some whole. In the case of a public monument that whole is the object in relation to its city. The vision of the artist must at all times embrace this synoptic whole. Ironically, Saddam Husain's monument is such a unity; it belongs to its city. But it is also overpoweringly vulgar, too literally and immediately transparent about its intentions to be art imbued with enigma and wonder. In Salim's monument the whole turns into a chronological narrative which might have worked as an artistic composition, but doesn't.

Instead of becoming the frame, or the way into the whole monument, the travertine-clad slab creates a spatial void which scatters instead of integrates and bears no relation to the elements themselves. It succeeds only in drawing attention to itself; from afar it becomes the missing *Gestalt* of the monument. The exquisite detail in the elements themselves (which shows how deeply the Assyrian tradition of wall-relief had been absorbed) is lost on the viewer because of the height. In a relief, the 'wall' being relieved is as much a part of the sculpture as the figures being 'released' from the wall, even when they are made from different materials. The play of background and foreground is what the whole thing is about, almost by definition. The voids and distances between figures need to be made and unmade *by the figures themselves*, inside their own self-created and self-contained world, whatever the content of its imagery. Instead, forms here are pinned up high like crucified butterflies in an entomologist's display case, their nuanced beauty and overall meaning lost in the harsh glare of the Baghdad sun.

Comparison with the compositional brilliance that leaps out from some of Salim's earlier small-scale relief work highlights what is missing in this one (Fig. 53); as would comparison with the work of that giant of the large-scale flat work Diego Rivera, who treated themes as panoramic and indigenous to Mexico as Jewad Salim's were to Iraq. Rivera was acutely aware of the problem of space, which is posed so differently in a monument as against a maquette or a canvas. He had learnt a fundamental lesson from Renaissance art; he had learnt to think like an architect and a painter at the same time.

But Jewad Salim was very special. By the early 1950s, he had forged a personal language, undeniably new, with which he created unforgettable images of daily life and ordinary people all set in a beautiful city of crescents and domes that has long since disappeared (Fig. 54). He tried many 'styles' and borrowed freely from the contributions of many of the great artists of the twentieth century (notably Picasso), all of which somehow ended up not as 'copying', but as stages in a search. A consistency of vision was finally achieved, elaborated not in words or heroic subject matter, but in the mundane formal language of all art: the language of line, form, space and colour. This was an artist who had something to say, and was filled with the urge to say it. Maybe the city of his images was never really there. In open-hearted hands nostalgia can be the engine of great artistic illusion. Such things don't matter. Was Edouard Manet's Paris of the 1860s and 1870s 'real'? More likely than not the powerful reality of 'Déjeuner sur l'Herbe' and 'Olympia' was not on the streets, but in the felt relations of Parisians with one another. When we look at

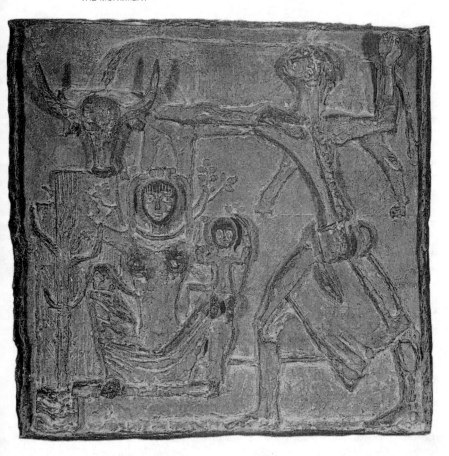

53. 'Man and the Earth', plaster relief, 45 cm x 45 cm. Jewad Salim, 1955.

Jewad's pictures and non-monumental sculptures, we sense that they add up to a new way of seeing. His measure as a great artist lies in the knowledge that like the Arabian nights and the hanging gardens of Babylon buried in the mists of time, his beautiful city and too-perfect heroes of everyday life, might just as well have been there.

However, real or not, Jewad Salim's city is now gone for ever, buried by Saddam Husain's regime and the cataclysmic avalanche of

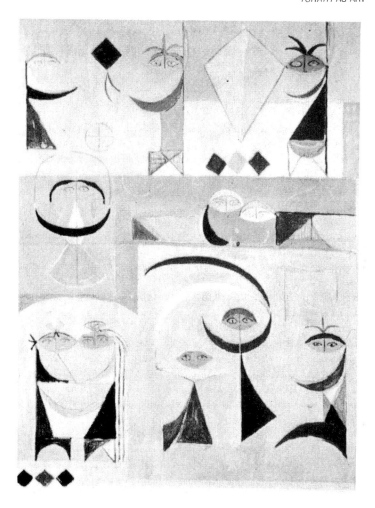

54. 'Children Playing', oil on canvas, 1953–4, Jewad Salim. Curved lines — invariably bright in colour — are used in this painting to convey movement and liveliness (as in the faces, eyes, limbs, skipping rope, balls, etc.). These elements are set against a typically modern orthogonally constructed perspectiveless background space painted in various hues of sandy yellows. The lozenge-shaped faces and exaggerated eyes are clearly Sumerian in inspiration.

mangled humanity in the Iraq–Iran war. While it might have been imaginable once, today it is unimaginable except in the form of the sweet and unforgiving lie. Art is not divided from kitsch merely by appearance, but by how each engages with the reality of the world it occupies. Salim was spared the loss of his city; his death at forty-one was an irreparable loss to Arab visual culture.

Salim's significance as an artist does not lie in the simplifications of those insatiable seekers of nostalgia in the name of *turath* who count themselves among his disciples; it lies in the fact that during the 1940s, from Paris and Picasso, to Rome and the Italian Renaissance, to London and Henry Moore at the Slade School of Art, Jewad Salim looked at the world with open eyes and an open heart. He understood that like the language of reason and 'common' sense, and unlike the language of speech, the language of vision is universal and belongs to everyone. The Arab world has many great works of applied art and architecture from antiquity onwards. But 'studio' art, and the professionalization of the business of how we see things, remained an unbroken tradition only in the West. The culture of *the word* is more than paramount in the Arab-Muslim world; it was actively pitted *against* the culture of the image in the Islamic injunction against figuration.[73] Poets, not painters, are the kings of Arab culture and always have been. Salim may have re-discovered the paintings of the thirteenth-century Arab painter al-Wasiti and the ancient traditions of Assyrian and Babylonian sculpture. But he did not do this by turning his back on that universal human 'language' of seeing things, a language which happened to have been forged largely in Europe. Impressionism, expressionism, cubism, constructivism, social 'realism', neo-plasticism, futurism, surrealism, pop, and everything else that ever happened to art will always be out there, waiting to be picked up, rejected or redeployed. From this standpoint no artist, whatever their nationality or cultural heritage, can ever again be anything but thoroughly 'international' in his or her origins. The lasting importance of Jewad Salim lies in the fact that he brought that language to a visually impoverished part of the world and created something new with it.

This is not how things came to be seen in Iraq. Salim's students, colleagues and followers in Iraq today have forgotten what he simply took for granted. Typically the intelligentsia reacts like Shams al-Din

Faris in *The Historical Origins of Wall-Relief Art in Modern Iraq*, who blames the 'new imperialism' for all artistic tendencies towards abstraction and away from realism. The insidious purpose of these tendencies, he claims, is to drive a wedge between the masses and their artists. Hitler used to make the same point over and over again in the late 1930s. For Faris, as for all Iraqis, Salim's was the epitome of a 'nationalist patriotic' art.[74]

Or it reacts with a meanness of spirit such as Shakir Hasan displays when he tries to 're-interpret' the too obvious fact that Jewad Salim greatly admired and learned from European sources and Henry Moore in particular. 'The reality is that we must trace the concerns of Henry Moore to the influences of ancient civilizations, in particular Mesopotamia.'[75] In other words, Moore does not have anything to offer an Iraqi artist in himself; and Jewad Salim was actually *seeing through him* back to his Mesopotamian origins.

Such thoughts are the initial steps towards a cultural narcissism of which Saddam Husain's vulgarity is the terrible culmination. The mythologizing of Jewad Salim was accomplished by denying the obvious non-Arab influences in his art, by believing that its value is linked to a 'national' cause, and by claiming that it is 'popular' in intent. But Salim's art owes as much to Henry Moore and Picasso as it does to Assyrian or Islamic art. His diaries in the crucially formative years 1938–46 have entries in four European languages, as though the artist, in seeking to record something that interested him, simply grabbed for one of the four languages he had taught himself in order to learn about Western art. The majority of artists today inside Iraq cannot stumble through an English newspaper; worse still, they don't feel his urge to look deeply into the interstices of cultures other than their own, cultures which have so obviously shaped the world they live in.

Salim first came to attention when his submission for the international competition for 'The Unknown Political Prisoner' in 1952 (Fig. 55) was among the eighty selected from some 3,500 entries to be exhibited at the Tate Gallery in London. His was the only Arab submission to win an award. In the following year he went on to make a tour of the United States which met with great acclaim. No other Arab artist of the 1950s received such international recognition, a recognition which ironically preceded any inside his own country.

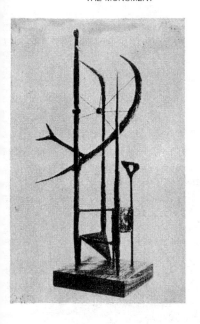

55. 'The Unknown Political Prisoner', plaster maquette, 1952. Jewad Salim's competition submission selected for special mention out of 3,500 entries from all over the world.

Strange Fruit

The 1961 monument to freedom is the watershed that marked the metamorphosis of Jewad Salim from an 'enemy of the people' in 1951, to the 'nationalist' and 'patriotic' Iraqi artist of today. Criticizing *nasb al-Hurriyya* is like praising Saddam Husain's monument; each in its own way does honour to *the* artist and *the* tyrant of Iraqi culture. Hero is to anti-hero as artist is to tyrant as Jewad Salim is to Saddam Husain. Or should it be the other way around? For a painter-sculptor to have achieved such status in an Arab-Islamic cultural tradition is no small feat. With respect, therefore, to both politics and the plastic arts, we have seen Iraq diverge from the norm in other Arab countries, for not a single one of them has ever bestowed such extraordinary status upon either a political leader or a visual artist, much less both at the same time.

The mythology that surrounds Jewad Salim and his 'pinnacle of achievement', the monument to freedom, may have begun with the

94

statement made by the Chairman of the Committee on the occasion of its unveiling.[76] But its persistence is attributable to other artists like Khalid al-Rahal, Shakir Hasan, Mohammed Ghani and the painter and art critic Jabra I. Jabra, all of whom count themselves among Salim's students, followers and most ardent admirers. They, not the politicians, are the human thread that binds art so tightly to kitsch in Iraq. When Salim died, Ghani who had been there all along (helping him in Italy to enlarge the maquette, and during the casting of the bronzes) worked tirelessly and indefatigably to finish the work. This was his apprenticeship for the later public commissions under the Ba'th.

Rifa'at Chadirchi, the highly respected architect of *nasb al-Hurriyya* and close personal friend of Salim, became Counsellor to the Mayor in 1980 and oversaw all the huge reconstruction projects of Baghdad. The design of the building so mindlessly repeated in Haifa street (see Fig. 14) is a variation on much better things designed by him in the 1960s. Hasan, Jabra, Ghani and Rahal had all been there from the very beginning as members of the 'Baghdad Group for Modern Art' set up by Salim in 1951 to create a new, identifiably Iraqi expression in art. Their work of earlier years showed a different kind of promise from that evident in the civic works of the 1980s (Fig. 56). So how could Jabra, who did more than anyone else to communicate the talent of Salim to a wider audience, present one sickly sweet, nostalgic and sentimental painting after another in his latest book, as examples of how far Iraqi art in the 1980s has come since and because of Jewad Salim (Figs. 57, 58)?[77] Of all people you would think he knows better. Strange fruit, it seems, was borne by the tree of freedom planted in 1958.

Then there is the case of Mohammed Makiya's Khulafa mosque completed on a tiny budget in 1963, only to be hailed as a masterpiece by the President in 1980 after he had suddenly acquired a new interest in religion and mosque design. At heart Chadirchi was a modernist; his interest in *turath* was always superficial (Figs. 59, 60). Yet in architecture, unlike painting and sculpture, there was a very rich heritage to work from; Makiya had been plumbing it since the 1950s, long before it became the thing to do. Commissioned to build a small mosque around a dilapidated ninth-century Abbasid minaret, the architect produced an outstanding building that was a first for its time

95

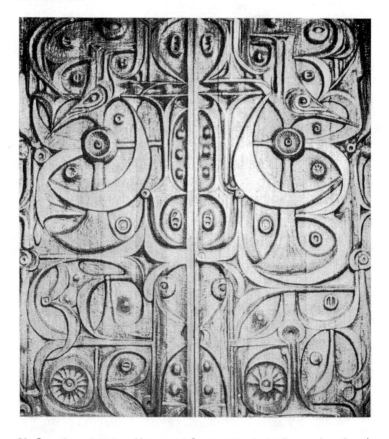

56. Carved wooden door, Mohammed Ghani, 1964. An intelligent adaptation of Arabesque motifs clearly influenced by Jewad Salim.

in Iraq (Figs. 61, 62). The ideas it encapsulated — of urban conservation, regionalism in matters of form, continuity of architectural heritage, respect for the local environment — had a considerable influence on a younger generation of architects many of whom studied under Makiya in the Baghdad School of Architecture.

In 1980, the year the war with Iran was launched, the Abbasid

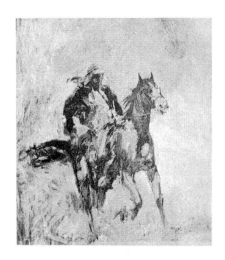

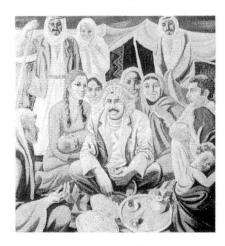

57. 'A Horseman', oil on canvas, 1980s, Faiq Hasan. Pure nostalgia produced for Ba'thi bureaucrats and Gulf shaikhs who want to be reminded of their noble Bedouin origins. Faiq Hasan was one of the great experimenters in Iraqi art. By the late 1940s he had already explored the visual possibilities of working with impressionist techniques and moved on to other things. Why is he returning to that technique in the 1980s? The answer is simple: money and an undue deference to popular taste.

58. 'The Struggling Leader Saddam Husain with the People', oil on canvas, 1980s, Mahood Ahmad. Another variation on the kitsch sensibility put forward by Jabra I. Jabra as an example of the best Iraqi art of the 1980s.

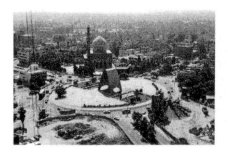

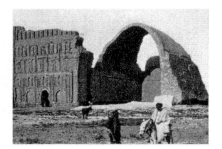

59. The old Unknown Soldier Monument in Sa'adoun square. Designed by Rifa'at Chadirchi. Built in the 1960s and torn down in the 1980s to make way for Khalid al-Rahal's monument on the same theme (see Fig. 17).

60. Ctesiphon arch just south of Baghdad (third century AD), the widest unreinforced piece of brickwork in the world, and obviously the inspiration behind Chadirchi's monument.

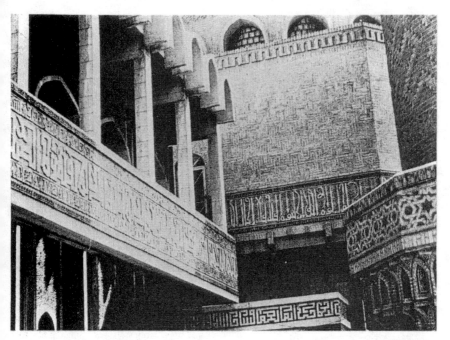

61. The Khulafa Mosque, Mohammed Makiya, 1963. A dynamic combination of old and new brick details. The base of the minaret can just be seen on the right.

tradition in architecture looked homegrown and was suitably Islamic. An extension to the Khulafa was commissioned. For once the site was not razed, and the new overblown mosque is layered on to the old, each layer standing in, as it were, for a different city (Fig. 63). Then came the Baghdad State Mosque competition, for a building to hold 30,000 people as against the fifty who can pray at any one time inside the 1963 Khulafa mosque. Makiya was asked to participate and the extreme monumentalism of his solution (Fig. 64) symbolizes the distance that the whole Iraqi intelligentsia had travelled from the unpretentious and more craftsmanlike days of the Khulafa.

Architectural projects and monuments now followed one another with bewildering frequency. And they became more and more grandiose. *Turath* had turned into a gigantic rolling stone which every architect

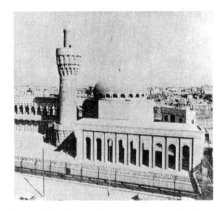

62. The Khulafa Mosque. The whole building can be viewed as a stage setting for the ninth-century minaret of al-GhazI.

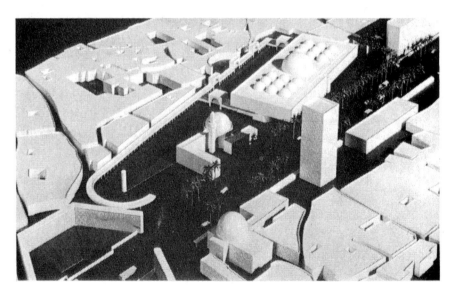

63. Proposed Khulafa Mosque Extension, The Architects' Collaborative, 1982. From real *turath* (the minaret) to *turath* as harmonious architectural art (the 1963 scheme) to *turath* as the unsympathetic overblown monumentalism of the 1980s. The only positive feature is the preservation of the different layers of the city in one scheme.

99

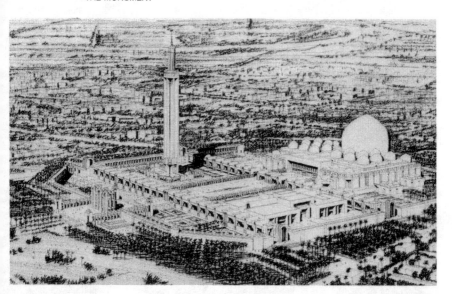

64. Baghdad State Mosque Competition, Mohammed Makiya, 1982. Compare with Robert Venturi's submission for the same competition, Fig. 35. Unlike Venturi's, this is a solution that genuinely derives from the Abbasid tradition; it does not playfully scrape at the outer trappings of shape and form but goes for the heart. Therefore it does not have Venturi's problems of meaning and one might even say that, for better or worse, it 'fits' its city perfectly.

and artist rolled along with. There is no point in listing their names: the best have already been mentioned; the rest only copied them.

A society which was really like a good poem, embodying the aesthetic virtues of beauty, order, economy and subordination of detail to the whole, would be a nightmare of horror for, given the historical reality of actual men, such a society could only come into being through selective breeding, extermination of the physically and mentally unfit, absolute obedience to the Director, and a large slave class kept out of sight in cellars.

Vice versa, a poem which was really like a political democracy − examples, unfortunately, exist − would be formless, windy, banal and utterly boring.

W. H. Auden, 'The Poet and the City'[78]

9
Singling Out
the Monument

Among all the monuments and art works of the 1980s in Baghdad, there is something breathtakingly terrible, beyond all notions of cause and reason, something finally incomprehensible and awful uniquely present in Saddam Husain's monument. Upon what is such a feeling founded? Does it need to be justified? At some level it is absolute, unshakeable and unjustifiable; it simply exists. Nonetheless, it needs to be explicated; to be elaborated upon and accounted for, and described over and over again in different ways. Why? Because finally the feeling must be judged.

Earlier chapters sought this terrible something in the appearance of the monument, in the way of making of the form, in its visible connectedness with state power and local kitsch. The exercise was one of visual archaeology, utilizing a language imposed by the monument, and taking the object as seriously as it takes itself; it was not an exercise in pure abstraction utilizing the monument as a mere stepping stone for the purpose of going somewhere else.

Now the problem is different; it is one of labelling that terrible something. Is it vulgarity? But to be *uniquely* vulgar is to stand out from the crowd in a way that destroys the meaning of the word. Then is it art? That is an even bigger problem because the monument is so intimately bound up with the way in which art became kitsch in Iraq. Saddam Husain made a fantastic piece of kitsch which incorporated an artistic insight in the casting of the arms. Unlike art, kitsch is unselfconsciously shared and created by a culture at large (Figs. 65, 66). Can a whole culture be complicit in some way in the production of such a monument? The distinctions between kitsch, vulgarity and art have to be *seen* if they are not to turn into figments of our imagination; they have to be present in the corporeal reality of the monument itself. On the other hand, the ineffable vulgarity of the monument as a singular whole, places question marks on all these distinctions. The fact is I no longer know by what standards to judge what it is I am looking at.

This kind of dilemma was not envisaged by Auden when he wrote 'The Poet and the City'; for in this wonderful essay the distinction between art and vulgarity was taken for granted. Being an artist was a moral vocation. Categories had meaning. Then Andy Warhol signalled that the categories which Auden took for granted were losing force. Robert Venturi did the same for architecture, and in doing so, revitalized its language, forcing the profession to question underlying assumptions and strike out in new directions. Post-Modernism, Deconstructionism and even the return to classicism in art and architecture were born from such transfusions between vulgarity and art. As a result we live now in a thoroughly relativized world; there are no universals, whether in the form of old-fashioned empires, essentialist theories of human nature, notions of progress through history, or 'ideal' philosophical systems which are anything other than historical curios.[79] Artistic opinions, even more than moral ones, can be anything these days.

Much of this has been liberating, particularly in the area of personal

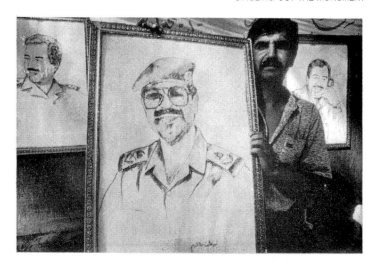

65. This man runs a small business selling portraits of Saddam Husain painted in his (the illustrator's) blood. It is disturbing to think that there is the same unselfconscious cultural-political sensibility at work in this scene as in the Monument itself.

choice and a flowering of different lifestyles. Culturally, it has introduced variety and cross-fertilizing influences. New fields of knowledge cutting across traditional disciplines have arisen (feminist and black cultural studies, for instance). Politically, it has been liberating for formerly colonized parts of the Third World. But intellectually, relativism has had damaging consequences. In particular, it has given currency to a defensive posture: the hiding behind pure feeling, the fear and avoidance of judgement. In art, the language these days is about 'liking' or 'not liking' things. You like it, it's art; you don't, it's not. The problem is that to be able to ask (much less answer) what are to my mind the truly fundamental questions about Saddam Husain's monument we are compelled to turn away from this kind of relativism, from feeling pure and simple, towards judgement that seeks a common ground.

Hannah Arendt, an isolated figure in Western thought, was never one for avoiding difficult questions. In her extraordinary book on the trial of Adolf Eichmann, she coined the phrase 'the banality of evil'.[80]

103

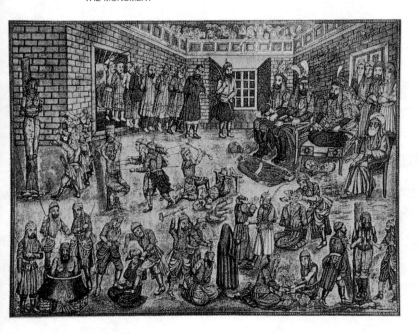

66. A popular and inexpensive Shi'i poster depicting scenes of torture in the afterlife inflicted upon the enemies of Husain, son of 'Ali. Date: early 1970s.

Arendt had attended the trial in the expectation of seeing something monstrous, 'radically evil' as she had earlier described it in *The Origins of Totalitarianism*. Instead she found out that Eichmann was an unusually dim-witted bureaucrat and sincere family man who spent a whole lifetime doing what he was told because that was all that he knew how to do. The evil that she had spent so much of her life trying to understand did not diminish in importance by the discovery that it was at some level banal in origin; it increased. Eichmann was too ordinary, too like so many other people; and that, in the end, is even more frightening. That was Arendt's point. She used 'the banality of evil' as a way of ridding herself emotionally of the idea of the incomprehensible, 'radical' nature of Nazi evil; the problem for her eventually turned into the much more humbling one of what we are all capable of doing in certain extreme situations.[81]

104

In the spirit of Arendt, can we compare the vulgarity of Saddam
Husain's monument to 'the banality of Eichmann's evil'? The answer
is going to depend on how kitsch and art, or vulgarity and the
incomprehensibly awful, meet in this object. Constantly, I find myself
tempted to use phrases like 'uniquely vulgar' or 'fantastic kitsch'.
Why? Certainly Eichmann was not 'uniquely banal'; the idea is
preposterous. On the other hand Saddam Husain stands out in ways
that Eichmann didn't. He is after all not a bureaucrat, but a ruler and
'maker' of his city, imbued with genuine authority.[82] His monument
stands out by comparison with others. It stands out even by
comparison with Hitler's victory monument (see Fig. 20), which is
after all only the Arc de Triomphe greatly enlarged. Hitler had a
complex about Paris; he wanted Berlin to be bigger and better. He
thought he could achieve this by copying the Arc de Triomphe (and
the Champs Elysées), while greatly enlarging it. The mindset behind
his arch is much easier to understand than the mindset behind Saddam
Husain's.

To return to the question: If Saddam Husain's monument poses the
question of evil, just as Eichmann's labours did, does it do so because
of its vulgarity, its kitsch-like quality, or insofar as it is something
incomprehensibly awful, as incomprehensible as a great work of art?
For that matter can a moral evaluation have shape, colour and texture?
Can it acquire physical presence? *Turath*-as-kitsch destroyed *turath*-as-art in Iraq. So what is art today in this small corner of the world?
And by whose standards of judgement? Can such questions be
answered? Certainly they must be asked.

Art and Plato's City

We feel comfortable with the idea that censorship, not kitsch or
populism, is the normal terrain on which art and tyranny meet.
Saddam Husain's monument could then be put aside as the bizarre
exception that it certainly is, and we can fall back on Auden's
certainties about art. Alternatively we can assume the indifference or
moral neutrality of art, as Warhol and Venturi do. Maybe then we can
look at the object 'objectively', without outrage, as though it were
something quaint. Art, after all, can flourish under a tyranny (for
example, the art of pharaonic Egypt, ancient Assyria, Islamic art in the

later centuries of political decline, and Italian art in the early years of Mussolini's dictatorship). Haven't the best architects always justified their commissions on the grounds that they are building for posterity?

Plato provides us with the first and still the richest account of how art, kitsch, vulgarity, beauty and morality acquire meaning in relation to one another through inextricable association with their city (in the Greek sense of polity, or city-state, and implying a cultural-political whole). Yet he did so not by standing in the shifting sands of a contingent world, but by himself creating a new Archimedian standpoint. He examined art and politics through the exception, which in his case was a city so impossibly perfect, it had to exclude Homer, Plato's favourite artist. Following in his footsteps, Rousseau did the same.[83] Both were wrestling with the central problem of this essay and neither suffered from an unwillingness to judge. Can the art of Plato be used to cast light on the creation of Saddam Husain? If so then maybe our humanity does have a medium with which to communicate across widely different cultures and through more than two thousand years of historical time.

Plato's city is not simply a 'place'; it is a well-ordered society, as neatly structured and balanced as Auden's good poem. Bigger than a family circle and smaller than humanity at large, Plato's ideal city is endowed with all the objectivity and concreteness of a work of art. It is an artefact, but one which like all cities has taken on the character of human necessity. It is an ordering of an otherwise arbitrary world into an intellectible whole incorporating habits, mannerisms, mores, social arrangements, institutional practices, notions of beauty, all of which must find themselves translated into urban rhythms, communication networks, public symbols and physical space (open and enclosed, private and public, large and small). Plato's city is never 'natural' or organic; it is the subjective become objective. When Aldo Rossi came along in the 1960s to recast our way of thinking about the city as a 'work of art', it is well to remember that he was following in these illustrious footsteps. Could it be that Baghdad and its inhabitants, Saddam Husain and his audience, the Republic of the Ba'th and its values, Iraqi art and Iraqi vulgarity, also all meet in Plato's city?

The underlying hypothesis of *The Republic* is that the city is the human soul writ large. To find justice in the soul, Socrates first looks for it in the city. The city is finally a regime with 'character', matching the soul which rules over it. As the regime changes so does the way of life of the whole city. Nothing is immutable. For Socrates civil society is the work of rulership, not the other way around. Civility itself (along with notions of vulgarity and art) is 'made' out of mores and laws as a craftsman manufactures an object. Even the 'nature' of human beings appears different from one society to the next, much more their tastes and aesthetic sensibilities. Human material may not be perfectible, but it is malleable. The art and way of life of the city changes with its kind of rule. To speak of the 'heroic culture' of ancient Greece, the 'effete decadence' of eighteenth-century France, the 'shoptrader commercialism' of nineteenth-century England, the 'arrogance' of Israel, the 'confessional mentality' of the Lebanese, the 'submissiveness' of the Egyptians, or the 'violent and sentimental' disposition of Iraqis, is to pay tribute to the Platonic idea that national-cultural traits are in some way related to the type of regime. From here it is but a short step to seeing how art and its nemesis, vulgarity, are also shaped by the regimes we are condemned to live in.

For Socrates a tyranny arises when the desiring part of the soul in a highly erotic (spirited) ruler runs amok. A tyranny *is* this rampant surge of an infinity of wants which the tyrant is driven by his *eros* to obtain with violence. Hence: a citizenry ruled by fear, uncertainty, wars and expansionism. Would Socrates describe the regime of the Iraqi Ba'th as a tyranny of this sort, as a regime in which desires were fulfilled in public which were better kept private or sublimated? This 'character' of Saddam Husain's regime can be reasonably inferred from the monument, from the fact that it seems graphically to capture, in splendid detail, the essential insatiability of all tyrants (bringing us back to the importance of the decision to cast the President's arms). Moreover, the hunger for an always illusory wholeness is perfectly captured in pan-Arabism, the legitimizing ideology of Ba'thism, which chafes at Iraqi boundaries as it strains for Arab unity. Is the personality of the Iraqi President reducible to an overcharged eroticism whose nature it is to hunger after base things? Is the Iraqi regime in some profound way dedicated to an unending search for what its leader and society at large find missing in themselves?

Plato's model of tyranny, however, is distinct from Iraq today, since by definition it has no art. Artists do not exist as insiders in the tyrannical city, whereas they exist in large numbers in the country of

Saddam Husain. In the tyrannical city, artists — like the person of Socrates in ancient Athens — exist on the fringes, as irritants, outsiders, whose fate invariably is neglect, exile, death. The artist in the unvirtuous city (which for Plato includes a democracy) cannot be an Andy Warhol; he is a rebel like Jewad Salim in 1951, more likely to be an 'enemy of the people' in his own lifetime. This, by the way, is also the only authentic artist recognized by Auden in 'The Poet and the City'.[84] Not even the desire to be an artist has a harmonious place inside Socrates' tyranny.

In Plato's ideal city, by contrast, the philosopher who was an outsider is in full control of the city. Necessarily, he is as erotically charged as his tyrannical counterpart; the difference is that the force of *eros* within him is married to reason (which for the Greeks included good judgement), not desire. Both the tyrant and the philosopher-ruler are ruthlessly singleminded men with a passion for wholeness, unlike the truly democratic individual who is easygoing, harmless, and does not take things very seriously (be it knowledge, power, sex or any other desire). In the ideal regime, authority rules inside the individual soul (everyone is contented with their place in the polity). And it rules over the sum of all souls in the shape of the philosopher-ruler.

The distinction between 'art' and 'philosophy' as we understand these words did not exist for Plato. His artist is more like a twentieth-century entertainer, a Michael Jackson catering to 'popular' tastes and passions. For him, truth was about virtue, and solely the business of philosophy. His artist looked to the manifold ambiguities of the human condition as he found it, not as it ought to be; he looked to opinion and 'imitated' nature or the makers of real things. Therefore, like Michael Jackson he dealt in phantoms or illusions of realities which others have created or played out in real life; such artists are not fabricators of reality themselves, Plato would say. They are imitators, and he despised them for this. Being concerned only with the outward appearances of things (not their inner truth, or 'good'), art merely reflects life in all its variety and contradictions as it is superficially, not as it really is deep down, which is also (in Plato's mind) how it ought to be. Nonetheless, the very act of artistic creation which imitates the base and the noble without choosing between them, is in itself an imitation of the act of rulership and therefore in competition with it over people's hearts. This is the fundamental source of the conflict between the city and the great artist. For rulers (like pre-Warhol modern artists) are the makers of real artefacts — real cities — not phantom images of drab reality. The nature of a maker, Plato argues, is to be guided by the good of what is being made, while the nature of art is imitation. Since the maker of a real thing is so obviously superior to his imitator, in the virtuous city the ruler is obliged to subject the artist to the overall good of the city. Homer will not be tolerated because his hero, Achilles, had too many human weaknesses to be a real model in the ideal city (he is proud, revengeful and sulks). The ruler needs an Achilles about whom only panegyrics are written and great hymns sung. Where will he be found?

Eventually Socrates leads his interlocutors into realizing what all religions later came to practise, namely, that in order for the city to live in justice, it must be founded on an original belief which Plato did not hesitate to call a great lie. The lie is an account of the origins of the city and its inequalities; it is a founding myth. Artists of a different ilk from Homer, Socrates says, are needed to create and make people believe in these poetic myths, which only their rulers know to be lies. No city can be without its heroes and stories of creation. In the ideal city, the artist is harnessed to the needs of the maker and in the business of spinning these out.

Significantly, however, Plato turns art into kitsch for the good of the perfectly just city not by violence — as in the city of the Ba'th — but by himself creating an extraordinary work of art. For the power of *The Republic* does not lie in its reasoning, but in its embodiment of what Auden called the 'aesthetic virtues'. The utopia it presents is as much a paradox as it is a solution to the problem of justice in the city. For Plato's republic is a terrible place, far worse than his tyrannical city; like a modern totalitarian state it places completely unreasonable demands on ordinary human beings. Ironically, even its philosopher-ruler is a very unhappy man. Plato lets us know that in order to be fit for the job of rulership, he has to want to be left alone to do philosophy. Therefore he would like to live in a democracy because it gives him the maximum amount of freedom to do what he wants to do. Held back by his knowledge of what is 'good' for his city, he reluctantly chooses public duty over private desire. But what exactly is his job?

To the pre-Warhol modern mind, it is Plato's philosopher-ruler —

not the strawman 'imitator' he has been setting up for us all along – who is the artist. The philosopher-ruler is a creator not an imitator, a maker of the most important work of art there can be: the city. For this task he or she has to be qualified, gifted, meticulously trained; in short the artist has to belong to an elite. Always he or she is guided by what is in the best interests of the work: how to achieve perfect justice in the city. Art for art's sake, you might say. Or politics as art. The quarrel between philosophy and mimetic art, which Plato resolved in favour of philosophy, now takes on curiously modern overtones. From the standpoint of this essay, it can be seen as a quarrel over the nature of artistic activity itself.

Truth is made, not found, and there can be no art that simply copies without aspiring to making truth. The 'useless' artefacts we call art today answer no need, unless it be the very need they themselves create. It was not always thus; the loss of belief in permanence, in endurance, in norms of human nature, in the significance of sensory phenomena, and the disappearance of what Auden called 'the Public Realm as the sphere of revelatory personal deeds', all this has changed the nature of art.[85] What we are left with is the quality of the truth that art makes. On the other hand, to have to live in that truth all the time, to have to live in Plato's city, is a 'nightmare of horror' as Auden rightly observed. Viewed through the prism of Ba'thi Iraq, therefore, the point of *The Republic* becomes the opposite of that which Plato made it appear to be: unless art is founded separately from politics, apart from prevailing morality, at a critical distance from all that is plebeian and popular in a culture, its truth self-destructs.

The Monument in Plato's City

Saddam Husain's monument was singled out because it symbolizes a wholesale breakdown in the ability to judge right from wrong. Looked at through the prism of Plato's city, the Iraqi ruler's creation acquires the attribute of being the quintessential kitsch object of that unhappy place in the 1980s, on a par with my favourite hot dog stand in Los Angeles. Being so special, the monument carries a message to all cultures that art cannot afford to be divorced from the judgement of what is art, nor morality from the judgement of what constitutes morality. 'Liking' or 'not liking' the monument has nothing whatsoever to do with such conclusions. The raw physicality of the thing says it all. Nonetheless, the message only becomes real to us today from within the special world of the Iraqi Ba'th. Plonk the monument in Trafalgar Square and it looks utterly bizarre, good for a laugh maybe. Robert Venturi didn't make sense in Baghdad either. Nor would Mohammed Makiya make sense in Las Vegas. Yet inside the Ba'thist city, this awesome moral symbol which calls itself art uproots the few remaining things our humanity has left to it today with which to assert its essential wholeness.

In Saddam Husain, we possess a rare thing: the still rational perfect tyrant whose art may or may not tower above society, but whose 'kitschness' is of that society's own making. Saddam Husain's monument teaches by practical example the important truth that Plato constructed in thought. For in the city of the Ba'th, art was not told to go into exile. Rather the line between it and kitsch was obliterated. The difference between these two things is the reason why, from the standpoint of art, the model for Saddam Husain's Iraq is Plato's ideal city, not his tyranny. Today in Iraq, the artists and the architects make kitsch, as well as the people and their rulers. There are no Jewad Salims; there is only Saddam Husain and artists like Khalid al-Rahal. No one who is obliged to live in such a place is immune. Plato's impossible city, not his run-of-the-mill tyranny, was founded in Baghdad.

Venturi destroyed an old language in order to create a new one, but Saddam Husain leaves only kitsch in his wake. Destruction without construction? Suppose it were so. What does it mean for a whole people? Imagine performing a frontal lobotomy on an otherwise normal brain with a view to permanently eradicating the 'artistic' component within, and you have some idea of the remarkable accomplishment of Saddam Husain with respect to modern Iraqi culture. Such an accomplishment reaches beyond the Republic of the Ba'th as it touches upon a wonder in the human condition itself, a wonder accessible to everyone wherever they live. Maybe, in the end this is the meaning of Saddam Husain's art and his vulgarity. Maybe it is the reason why in Ba'thi Iraq there is no longer any intelligent way of distinguishing between the two, no way of telling good art from bad, all art from kitsch, or what is right from what is wrong. If so,

111

then reasonable human beings must ponder the remarkable fact that such a state of affairs has become possible.

From *Turath*-as-Art to *Turath*-as-Kitsch: a Historical Sketch

Kitsch and art in Iraq meet in a growing historical obsession with the self: whether it be the sickening 'I' of Saddam Husain (the rise of his leadership over all organs of party and state culminating in his Presidency and the 1979 purge of the Revolutionary Command Council), or the endlessly mystifying 'we' of *turath*, born long before the Ba'thi republic of 1968.

The art of Jewad Salim attained its pinnacle of achievement within an artistic 'spirit' that found a rich source in *turath*. His work spoke to a whole generation; it was simultaneously typical and not typical of them. From the 1940s visual culture and society had evolved in a typically dynamic and healthy tension between the old and the new. All realities (political, social, cultural) tended to be placed under critical scrutiny. The rebellious spirit of modernism dominated, even though (or maybe because) the visual reappropriation of *turath* was the artistic heart of this spirit.

In 1958, revolution, mass movements, political experimentation, unease, reaction and military rule set in. The space between politics and culture began to shrink. Popular culture rose in importance, and culture itself as an aloof, professional and critical enterprise began to give way to propaganda. The state became acutely aware of the need to have a much greater role in culture making. Between 1958 and 1968, cultural production in all areas became revolutionary and propagandistic, while remaining critical and idealistic. But it was no longer as deep. A work like the Freedom Monument epitomizes these strengths and weaknesses (think of the idealism of the message, Salim's need to compromise, the loving attention to sculptural detail, the failure of the whole). The death of Jewad Salim as he worked on the final stages of a monument commissioned by a military junta, however popular, foreshadowed the end of a rich period in the history of Iraqi art.

But the real end came after 1968. The Ba'th carried mere tendencies from the previous decade to something like a logical extreme, a twisted version of Plato's Republic. In their hands *turath* was an ideology as well as a weapon. The longing for identity that it represented in the face of an initially justifiable fear of the uprooting march of modernity, had already been politically forged in their pan-Arabism (the first Ba'thi student circles in Iraq started in the late 1940s). But carried to an extreme (and in the sphere of politics, not art), this ordinary, all too human fear swelled up into hate and bristling suspicion of the outside. The whole world, welcomed at first with open arms (witness the reactions of nineteenth-century Arab travellers to Europe, or Jewad Salim's joyous discovery of Western art), now presented itself in paranoid garb, filled with enemies of Arabism and agents of Imperialism and Zionism. (Remark, for instance, the manic search for spies and the flood of conspiracy trials in Iraq between 1968 and 1973.)

The idea of unity – whether pan-Arab or Islamic – played the same metaphysical role in Arab culture as the tradition of organicism and a return to nature in romantic Western thought. In both, an illusory hunger for wholeness is at work, originating in a deep hostility (albeit contradictory) to the pluralistic, fragmented, schizoid, individualized nature of modernity. Invariably the cosmopolitan, fragmented city of strangers which mushrooms everywhere in the early stages of modernization, is perceived as threatening and a focus of attack. (American romantics of the nineteenth century had a very acute case of this as they faced the post-civil war expansion of their cities.[86]) Just as their equivalents had done in the West, Iraqi romantics like Jewad Salim achieved things in art; but they did so by focusing on *turath* not on nature. (By contrast, the romantic temperament in thought and politics starts from a huge liability; the writings of Michel 'Aflaq, founder of the Ba'th, being a case in point.[87])

The hold of the Ba'th over the culture was born long before the party came to power. The ideas which eventually served to legitimize their power were hegemonic in society in the 1960s. If this were not so, the startling success of Ba'thism in Iraq and Syria would be inexplicable. The innermost assumptions of Iraqis about politics, human nature, the structure of the world, who their friends and enemies are, all these must be judged to have had something to do with that success. Romanticism in art and romanticism in politics met in Iraq in the shape of the twenty-year-old Ba'thi regime. Nonetheless, it

113

must be emphasized that logically they didn't have to. Other *outcomes* could have emerged from the cauldron that was Iraq in the 1950s and 1960s. And the nature of politics is like art, in that a new beginning is always in principle possible. Precisely because there was no necessary conjunction between art and politics in Iraq, the contingent steps by which that meeting came about, and our judgement of the outcome, are two entirely separate things. The judgement that all-art-became-kitsch in the Baghdad of the 1980s is therefore about 'what is art'; it is not about historical processes.

By contrast with the 1940s and 1950s, the culture the Ba'th have created in Iraq is wholly state-produced and 'imitative' of its ruler's wants and desires. The artist has become the fashionmonger that Plato only posited him to be. No longer is there any critical distance, either from the state or from that fundamental and founding myth of the Ba'thist city, 'the people'. Populism and the idea of a culture for the masses (which ended up as kitsch and propaganda) rules intellectual and artistic production in Iraq. The interiorized,

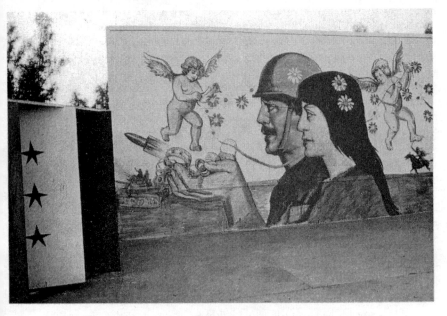

67. A wallposter that appeared during the Iraq-Iran war

xenophobic world of the Ba'th is taken objectively, narcissistically, without any consideration of alternatives, of what things are like on the 'outside', or even of ideal 'other' possibilities. Mythical reconstructions of the Baghdad and Babylon of Saddam Husain and Nebuchadnezzar, have become elaborate lived-in fantasies, surreal wish-dreams which are fine as kitsch, but something else entirely when acted out in real life. I may enjoy Salvador Dali, but I certainly don't want to live in his paintings, any more than I am able to live in Saddam Husain's Baghdad. We all may be 'such stuff as dreams are made on', but the moment Saddam Husain turned his dreams into the city of all Iraqis, he snuffed out art and invested kitsch with a totalizing sovereignty (Fig. 67).

If the beauty of virtue were the product of art, virtue would
have long since been disfigured.

Jean-Jacques Rousseau[88]

10
Ethical Ambiguities

By and large an entire generation of Iraqi intellectuals collaborated
with the Ba'thist regime in Iraq. Consider the case of someone like
Khalid Rahal. Why did he assist the President on his monument? His
early work suggests that he knew better. Fear, and the self-serving
opportunism that it breeds, are the simple answers. However, even in
such a public climate it is still not possible to take away from citizens
all zest for life simply because the fear of death has been placed
uppermost in their minds. On the contrary this same fear compels
them jealously to guard and protect their loved ones at the expense of
everything else. What is a work of art under these conditions? Why art
in the first place? To whom is an artist responsible for his or her

work? These are existential questions for artists living inside Iraq today.

The novelty of Iraqi conditions from the cultural point of view, is that an artist's zest for life is steeped in an ocean of meaninglessness. Fear dispels hope and engenders an awareness of mortality so palpable and personalized that the very idea of the 'immortality' and permanence of art becomes unreal or a public charade. From within the world of fear, opportunism rules behaviour; from within the world of hopelessness, cynicism rules intelligent thought. Never is there a justification for art in itself; survival is all that counts. The more things apparently changed for the better as far as art was concerned (in terms of number of commissions, the rising status of the artist, the amount of state resources allocated to cultural production), the more acute became the real pointlessness of all art in Iraq.

The Responsibility of the Artist

Extraordinary conditions do strange things to the moral universe of art. They impose a more intense kind of responsibility upon the artist towards himself and others (spouse, children, friends, fellow citizens), the nature of which is to shackle the imagination. Under conditions of rampant fear, the last thing people care about is the quality of art and the ethical environment in which it is produced. However, these conditions which undermine art even as they absolve the artist do not make the problem of responsibility easier; they make it harder.

Is artistic responsibility during the act of creation inwardly focused or outwardly directed? After Fascism and Stalinism, we think we know a great deal about what happens when the arts are subjected, or subject themselves, to a 'national' or state ideology as has now happened in Iraq. But the re-emergence of classicism in the plastic arts, and the re-evaluation going on in many circles of the art and architecture produced in Germany and Italy in the inter-war period, should make us think again. Some of the best Iraqi artists held the belief that they were somehow 'responsible' to the nation as a whole. To the post-war Western mind political freedom and the flourishing of the arts are seen as natural corollaries, which they have not been in previous centuries – certainly not in Iraq where the very idea of a

117

monumental or urban art was born in close association with absolutist states.

Paradoxically, in a smoothly functioning tyranny (but not in Plato's totalitarian utopia), citizens can sometimes afford to 'let themselves go' in ways which in a politicized free society they cannot afford to do. Freedom demands self-restraint; it imposes a new kind of public responsibility as some artists in the newly liberated countries of Eastern Europe are finding out. The artist in a tyranny is an unconstrained outsider, who is sometimes even left alone or allowed self-exile. To be suddenly thrust into exhilarating freedom can be very disorienting. On the other hand, if a citizenry has become apolitical for whatever reason (as in an ageing democracy), then public life can become positively boring. Both boredom and a strong sense of public responsibility debilitate the artistic impulse, which in at least some aspect, large or small, itches to break with convention. In a self-complacent and perfectly respectable society, with no outlaws and no rebels, or in a society where nothing matters because absolutely everything is permissible, wants, passions and desires either become moderated or they find themselves ventilated wantonly, irrationally: a theme explored in Anthony Burgess's novel *A Clockwork Orange*. Tyrannies by contrast cultivate the extremes; they fuse the indispensable inwardness and heightened passions of the artistic spirit with a powerful outward sense of purpose. This is what is most memorable about the underground literature that came out of Latin American dictatorships or Eastern Europe after the extremes of Stalinist terror had abated.

But in general, Western culture is more secure with the thought that responsibility is inwardly focused. When an artist subjects him or herself willingly, introducing ideology or any moral idea as a constraint upon creation just like any other constraint (the canvas of a painter, the material of the sculptor, the instrument of the musician or the needs of users), art of lasting value can be produced. Propaganda art, like patriotic poetry or moralizing literature, fails as art when the end it is intended to serve takes over from *the way of making* of the artefact. When this happens, the interiorized world of art has been disregarded for the sake of some outer value extrinsic to its making, like 'the Leader', 'the people', some idea, or financial remuneration. Sociability will now rule supreme in the very crucible of creation — the domain of making — to the certain detriment of art (Figs. 68, 69).

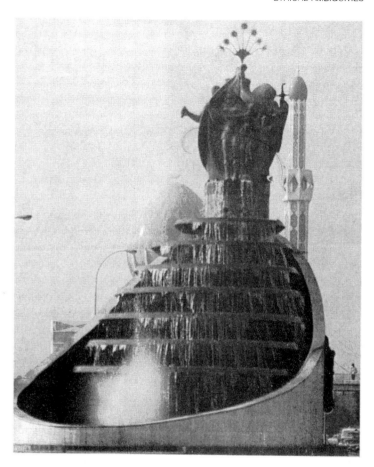

68. 'The March of the Ba'th', a monument in Mathaf square, Baghdad, by Khalid
Rahal. Commissioned in 1973. 35 metres high x 15 metres wide. The bronze figures
are contained within what the official government paper, *Al-Thawra*, 23 April 1987,
describes as 'the voyaging ship which carries within it the experiences of the nation
and its yearnings for the future'. Compare this with Rahal's earlier work, Fig. 69, and
the Unknown Soldier Monument of the 1980s, Fig. 17. The artistic degeneration is
glaringly evident. But where exactly does it lie? Technically, he is as proficient as ever.
But the triumphalist clichés of 'The March' are starting to crowd in the form: little
plaques full of messages are actually plastered all over the concrete walls of the 'boat'
on the side facing the mosque. The ability to say something original through form alone
is almost lost. By the time we get to the Unknown Soldier Monument, the cliché is
everything.

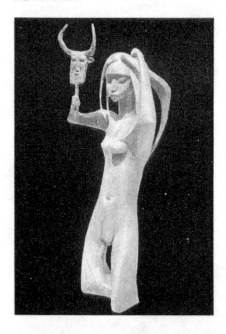

69. 'Sharqawiyya' (Arab girl from southern Iraq), Khalid Rahal. Early 1960s.

This is what happened to the weakest section of Jewad Salim's 1961 monument, the centrepiece, which depicts a soldier bursting through prison bars (Fig. 70). In this isolated instance in the Freedom Monument, art was subordinated to the need to secure an important commission. (The new military government accepted the soldier as a compromise symbol for the army's role in the 1958 revolution; they had wanted the image of Brigadier 'Abdul Karim Qassem. Salim wanted neither but accepted the former.) By contrast the art in Saddam Husain's monument arises from a way of making — casting — uniquely suited to the horrific political intent of the work.

Art doesn't fail because the artist's message or the moral idea behind the work is bad, just as it doesn't fail because we don't agree with the artist. For instance, I don't like Plato's utopian city or agree with his imitation theory of art. But *The Republic* is so richly constructed as to render that irrelevant. I can use the work to draw other conclusions. This is impossible to do with propaganda art. The point of art always is to have something to say, and a self-made and therefore deeply felt way of saying it. Rahal, Ghani and all the others stopped having something to say a long time ago, and so turned into technicians. Art is made to happen, or not happen as the case may be, because of the relation between these two things, a relation which has to be present in the object itself (not invented in the mind, as in so much of what passes for art these days).

Maybe, then, the progress of the arts is bound up with the view that whatever the artist does must in the end be for the good of the whole. Could the very uselessness of art, its disengagement from sociability and preoccupation with the good of the artefact, be the source of its value? One of the professional hazards of being an artist is the espousal of this ideology, whether in the form of utopian social blueprints, 'art for art's sake', or absolute positions regarding freedom of expression. A romantic like Shelley, for instance, went so far as to say that the greatest poets were necessarily 'men of the most spotless virtue' whose sins 'have been washed in the blood of the mediator and redeemer, Time'.[89] The beauty of this position is that it rids us completely of the whole problem of responsibility. It is enough simply to be an artist (or an architect working for a tyrant whose commissions are justified by an unknowable future).

Better than most, however, Shelley knew that the very act of imagining evil in art (a great novel like *Crime and Punishment*, for instance) presumes a brooding kind of intimacy with the real thing. An artist's knowledge of his creations is 'through inclination or congeniality', as Maritain put it, and even when he creates a character whom he genuinely despises, then he does so with the kind of lucidity 'which makes a man know his enemy as himself'.[90] Is it possible to deploy such knowledge in the form of art without being complicit in some small way in whatever awful thing is being depicted? For that matter is it possible to make propaganda art, however cynically, without becoming complicit in the propaganda itself? Certainly that is not the lesson of Saddam Husain's monument. Even if the meaning of the monument were to be transformed in the fullness of time, by becoming a testament to terrible memories, for instance, why should its maker be redeemed? Shelley has confused the work with its human agency. Jewad Salim was a great artist, responsible only to himself. But has his work truly been redeemed in the culture which once reviled it? For that matter is it properly appreciated as art? If not, then what is at the root of this artist's status in Ba'thi Iraq?

121

Suppose the responsibility of an artist originated in the fact that the experience of art is prior to the production of the work. It is not the function of the artist simply to have personal experiences, but to create them for others. That is, so to speak, his or her job. The experience, in itself, is a private affair, and it behoves artists to have as many of them as possible and as intensely as they know how, or can afford to get away with. However, in order to enjoy art, or have any relation to it at all, a public of non-artists, ordinary Iraqi citizens, must also have such experiences to one degree or another.

Now the technical skill of being an artist becomes one of 'objectifying' the experience, ripping it out of one's own private self and giving it a separate physical identity which a public can henceforth engage with. Ironically, therefore, the *better* the artist, the *greater* the responsibility because the more powerful is the ultimate impact of the object of art on larger numbers of people who are usually remote from the artist (in place, time and circumstance). At this point not only has the personal-moral life of the artist begun to impinge on art, but, at the limits, there even arises what the Catholic philosopher Maritain, thinking of Oscar Wilde, Cocteau and André Gide, has called 'the temptation of a merely artistic morality'. He has in mind the fascinating business of exploring new human horizons by knowingly experimenting with 'one's own soul and body and with the destiny of other human beings', of 'heroically plunging into evil in order to redeem it by poetry'.[91] This is the extreme that proves that the tension between the morality of the community or the demands of sociability and the aesthetic drive of individuals is probably in the end always irreconcilable; it is not the extreme of Saddam Husain's monument.

Plato and Rousseau employed such a view of the responsibility of the artist to ban Homer and Molière from their ideal cities. On the grounds of a radical separation between virtue and art, Rousseau, like Plato before him, opted for the former against the latter in his great polemic against the Enlightenment. The fact is they got it right, and Shelley is the one who got it wrong. Virtue, like wisdom about human concerns in general, does have another source wholly divorced from art. The romantic temperament which prevailed among the Iraqi intelligentsia (until it went cynical, opportunistic and sour under the Ba'th) will always find this subversive truth hard to accept. For it turns the artist into the true individualist, always the pariah and the

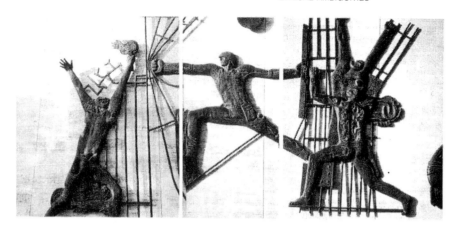

70. The centrepiece of *nasb al-Hurriyya* (the Freedom Monument), Jewad Salim, 1961.

elitist, anything but the populist. Rousseau and Plato were not afraid of any threat posed to the virtue of their city by the mediocre or average artist; they were afraid rather of the threat posed by *the most responsible* kind of artist (towards art). Why? Because the commitment to art is itself a virtue, even though the principal concern is with the good of the work, not the good of humankind. Sincerity, purity, dedication, curiosity, self-sacrifice, are virtues which the artist must be prepared to apply to his work when the work demands it of him. Strangely these are *imitations* of the virtues expected of human beings in a community.[92] But they are not the same thing; to be dedicated in the making of an object is not to be self-sacrificing towards another human being. Virtue is not, nor can it ever be, art. It is the supreme irony of *The Republic* that Socrates (after whom Plato's ideal philosopher-ruler is modelled) had to die because his commitment to philosophy stood above his commitment to his city, which, after all, had only asked of him to repudiate philosophy. And Homer was dangerous to Plato's city because vice is present in his poetry with the same undistinguishing grace as virtue. So it was with Molière who in *The Misanthrope*, according to Rousseau, used his art to poke fun at virtue. On the horns of this strangely posed dilemma, much of political and moral philosophy was conceived.

123

Plato's way of looking at responsibility, like art for art's sake and romanticism, arises from within the domain of the artistic impulse itself. It implies a kind of responsibility which can be, and frequently is, ruthless on the artist or on the people dearest to him (the case histories are legion: Gauguin, Van Gogh, Frank Lloyd Wright, Munch, Rivera, Picasso, and today Salman Rushdie). The artist insofar as he or she really is an artist has ends which prioritize the good of the work, not real life or how it is lived. He or she is an idolater in the truest sense of the word. On the other hand, to prefer the good life over the good object, as Plato and Rousseau did, is to relegate the whole activity of art to a secondary place in the human scheme of priorities.

The kindest thing that can be said about the collaboration of the Iraqi intelligentsia in the various works of the Ba'thist city is that they chose *to live* at the expense of their art or whatever else they were engaged in doing. In the conditions of Iraq that is an obvious but by no means an easy choice to make. Faced up to honestly, with the minimum of necessary compromises, and with the interests of loved ones in mind, it can actually become heroic. There are many such heroes in Iraq today. Any other kind of choice (Jewad Salim's, for instance, which is based on the primacy of the artefact) would, under the regime of Saddam Husain, have resulted in a nameless and even stupid death, one in which even the extreme option to die heroically or 'artistically' (as in the case of Mishima, the Japanese writer and poet), or even simply to live 'for art', is taken away from people. Being an artist or any other kind of hero no longer exists as an option (extreme or otherwise) in a place like Ba'thist Iraq. By the same token, it must be acknowledged that by and large the works that such an intelligentsia produces are worthless.

To adopt Plato's notion of responsibility is to magnify the moral responsibility of the artist. The unrelenting artist is no longer faced with choosing between being an artist or giving it all up for other people's sake; he or she is alone, left (like Salman Rushdie) dangling on the hook of his or her own art. Or as alone as Saddam Husain would be were we to have finally judged his monument a genuine work of art. Then and only then would we have no one else to blame for this monument but this one man. Certainly we could not find fault with those like Khalid Rahal who were compelled to assist him.

But Saddam Husain's monument is not in the end a work of art because of its vulgarity and roots in local kitsch. It calls itself art but refuses to bow down before any canon of artistic taste. Ruthlessly the monument weeds out all the false quasi-artistic gestures of the so-called professionals and thus succeeds in defining them on its own terms rather than being defined by them. This is not how kitsch is supposed to work. But then the prism of Saddam Husain's monument inverts and degrades everything. If I have written about the art of the monument, it is only to highlight the rule of vulgarity, the demise of art and the complete moral breakdown of public culture. But none of these were intended outcomes. The Ba'th see themselves as pioneering a *renaissance* of Arabic culture (the literal meaning of the word *Ba'th*). An artist, however, can be intentionally vulgar, can want to subvert art by elevating kitsch. This was the lesson of Andy Warhol and Robert Venturi. Remove intentionality and what is left of responsibility? Put differently, who is responsible for the vulgarity of Saddam Husain's monument? Who is responsible for the fact that it is such a fantastic piece of kitsch?

Collective Responsibility

According to *The Oxford English Dictionary*, 'vulgar' is an adaptation of the Latin *vulgaris* formed on the notion of 'the common people'. When a thing is vulgar, this means it is 'in common or general use', or that it is 'of or pertaining to the common people'.[93] Moreover, kitsch, as we have seen, is an unselfconscious sensibility, necessarily shared by large numbers of people.

By implication, therefore, the notion of responsibility which is posed in the above question is a collective one, not pertaining to individual intentions, even when that individual happens to be an absolute ruler. How do we deal with the extremely disturbing idea that the notion of responsibility which ought properly to be invoked in the case of Saddam Husain's monument is a collective and not an individual one?

The fact of human interconnectedness, not the desire to ascribe blame or find fault, is at the origin of the notion of collective responsibility.[94] The resources of a country, nationhood, the quality of

125

citizenship, are indivisible goods which bring harm or benefit to everyone not as individuals, but as members of one collectivity. Communities are held together by facts of geography, language, psychology, and a common history and destiny. People's ideas, habits, mores, feelings of vicarious pride and shame — in ancestors, country, religious group — all accumulate over generations to create a discernible moral and cultural order within a community which differs from that of another. One can say about the British, for instance, that they are still 'insular' in their attitude to Europe; about the French that they 'like' centralization in government, and so on.

Thus democracies establish and are established by certain generalized habits and practices, as are tyrannies or even societies with very weak state allegiances like the Lebanon. In the Iraqi popular imagination the rule of Saddam Husain finds an analogue in the notoriously draconian rule of al-Hadjadj ibn Yusuf al-Thaqafi (694 AD); both originate in clichés about how the Iraqi national character 'asks' to be ruled. Whatever the validity of such clichés, their very presence renders them part of the Iraqi cultural-political reality. If a trait like insularity, or a propensity for harsh government, exists as a contingent or historically explicable fact which cannot rationally be reduced to a mere sum of the traits of the individuals concerned (not all British are insular, nor are all Iraqis unruly hotheads), then a non-distributive form of 'collective responsibility' for that trait (good or bad) can also be reasonably deemed to exist.

Nor do I have to resort to any kind of metaphysics to postulate the reality of collective responsibility and make sense of statements about an entity called 'Iraq'. However, I do have to believe, as Valéry once put it, that if I were all alone in the world, I would be incapable of inventing everything that my will 'commands' me to do because of the inescapable fact that I share that world with others. When is my 'will' mine, and when does it belong to someone 'other' than me whom I have allowed to be imposed on myself? If the latter (at least some of the time) then even my freedom to act is not, strictly speaking, mine all of the time. It belongs to a collective 'other' with real substance. I cannot entirely escape my association with it or responsibility towards it any more than I can escape responsibility towards myself.

Kitsch and vulgarity, unlike artistic originality, are broad cultural outcomes of human action which demonstrate the existence of this 'other' will acting through me. As phenomena they are not simply an amalgam of individual actions; they are independently constituted *sui generis* forms. The notion of their belonging to a landscape made by an entire community of people, who are therefore 'responsible' for what that landscape looks like, must be as valid as those phenomena are real.

A profound maxim of secular moral philosophy is that guilt, and therefore at least one kind of responsibility, does not transfer. We always protest, as Paul Valéry rightly says, against prolonging moral responsibility beyond the term of the individual on whom it devolves.[95] But neither the law (for instance on war reparations, certain types of liability or parental obligations) nor our everyday ways of thinking are always consistent with this important principle. Companies are responsible for the embezzlements of their employees. What parent has not felt guilty or responsible for shameful behaviour on their children's part, however old? And who is responsible for the Israeli policy of indiscriminate beatings and demolition of houses in the Occupied Territories, actions carried out by a duly elected government supported by a majority of its population? One kind of response unhesitatingly speaks of an 'Israeli' responsibility for these actions, as it speaks of a white South African responsibility for Apartheid, an American responsibility for the deforestation of Vietnam, and a Nazi German responsibility for the Holocaust.

But the inconsistency between the moral principle (that responsibility does not transfer from one individual to another) and these examples arises not because the principle is wrong, but because in its very essence *responsibility is singular in kind* and *untransferable* between kinds. Individual responsibility does not transfer to other individuals nor does it transfer to the collective. And the obverse is equally true: collective responsibility does not transfer to the individual. The hardest thing in the world of course is to know which is which and where to draw the line, but that at least is a formal problem (legal and political) which presumes the existence of more than one kind of responsibility.

The principle of collective responsibility is legislatively recognized and systematically practised inside Iraq (for instance, against the Kurds). The public at large expects and is accustomed to the idea of the separation of fault from liability in circumstances that are unacceptable elsewhere in the world (for instance, the regular occurrence inside Iraq of entire families being held responsible for actions which the state itself ascribes to only one member). Feinberg is, therefore, wrong in his view that 'the changes that have come with modern times have dictated quite inevitably that the one principle [individual responsibility] replace the other [collective responsibility], and no "alternation" is remotely foreseeable, unless massive destruction forces the human race to start all over again in tiny isolated farming settlements'.[96] Modernity, it seems, comes in all shapes and forms; 'history' has not 'dictated' that punishment be tied to individual responsibility in Iraq.

The question of responsibility has to be posed completely differently in a state ruled by fear than it would be in an ordinary state because on the whole the populace does not *feel* itself responsible for the actions of its rulers, even when it *knows* that momentous life and death decisions are taken in its name (like starting and stopping the bloodiest war in the modern history of the Middle East). At least there was an anti-war movement in the United States (which forced an end to the Indo-Chinese war), and there was a 'Peace Now' movement in Israel after the latter's invasion of Lebanon. When the 'collective' is so split within itself, then, by the same token, a 'collective conscience' of sorts is at work. No such conscience is able to exist today in Iraq.

At the same time that Saddam Husain's monument was being cast in Britain, a massive army campaign to eradicate Iraqi Kurds with poison gas was under way. The war had ended and Kurdish guerrillas in the mountains did not constitute a threat. Anyway the gas was directed at villages, towns and fleeing populations trapped in mountain passes and the like. Later in the summer of 1988, it was turned on some thirty thousand apolitical army deserters who had collected in the last years of the Iraq–Iran war in the marshes of the south.[97] Such weapons have to be made in factories, transported in trucks, and dropped by yet other parties from the air. Since 1968 political detainees have been regularly 'disappearing' in captivity, or have been given heavy metal poisons in their drinks on the day of release so as to die a slow and grisly death in unsuspecting freedom (chemical weapons have a much longer ancestry in Iraq than is suggested by the headlines of the late 1980s). Hundreds of thousands of people had to join the Ba'th party and the security services to carry out these policies. And the whole country participated in the biggest war of its history without so much as a whisper of protest for eight gruelling years.[98] The peculiarity of the Iraqi regime therefore is to have involved enormous numbers of people directly in its crimes over twenty years, while making the rest of the population at the very least complicit in their commission. Yet, everyone inside the country, including the opposition outside, denies all responsibility for what they know has been going on. Even if an Iraqi is prepared to recognize the above as crimes (not matters of 'national security') he will become outraged at the charge of complicity.

Is a person responsible if he does not feel responsible? Responsibility, in the Occidental tradition of ethics, must be acknowledged; people must be under the burden of their freely made choices, choices made in the light of knowledge of the consequences. Responsibility, therefore, is inwardly directed. But this is not the case in the Islamic tradition which construes responsibility as a duty directed not towards oneself but outwardly, towards an 'other' will outside the self. And it is not the case in Ba'thi Iraq. 'Where all are guilty, nobody in the last analysis can be judged. For that guilt is not accompanied by even the mere appearance, the mere pretence of responsibility.'[99]

If the pilots who dropped canisters of poison gas on defenceless Kurdish families are *guilty* (in the sense that there is no doubt, even in the minds of the perpetrators, about who dropped the canisters), are they nonetheless *responsible* for the ensuing dead, having merely acted on orders from above on pain of certain death if they refused? What about those Iraqis who espoused Arab nationalism in earlier years? Or those who actively and voluntarily supported the Arab Ba'th Socialist Party in its post-1958 ascent to the forefront of Iraqi politics? Like the Germans who voted Hitler into office, they are *responsible* for legitimizing the authority and power behind Saddam Husain, and this in the end made his later policies possible. But it is ludicrous to think that this makes them *guilty* of those later crimes, any more than a run-of-the-mill German nationalist of the 1930s can be deemed to be as guilty of the Holocaust as those who managed and operated the gas ovens. The Iraqi intelligentsia collaborated wholesale with Saddam Husain in the making of his city. Khalid Rahal *made* Saddam Husain's monument. But he wasn't responsible for making it. No one had any choice in the matter. So what does all of this do to the idea of a 'collective responsibility' for Saddam Husain's vulgarity and his kitsch?

Excising the Monument

Monuments are more than aesthetic objects. In their deepest essence they are about memories, memories that constitute the very marrow of a city's identity, bestowing personality and character upon a city just as they do upon an individual. The form, shape, size and way of making of a monument, the story of how it came to be there, the trials and tribulations of those who made it, the manner of its placement in its city, all of these contribute to crystallizing the workings of memory. For these purposes it does not matter whether those memories are good or bad. But it does matter how they relate to their city, and which monuments survive to represent them. It is here that the question of responsibility — individual or collective — arises.

All over Eastern Europe monuments were being torn down in 1989, just as they were torn down in Hungary in 1956. When the statues of General Maude and King Faisal I were brought down in Baghdad on the morning of 14 July 1958, angry people thought they were excising the bad memories of the British Mandate and monarchical rule (Fig. 71). Thirty-one years later, on the anniversary of that event and only three weeks before the opening ceremony for his very own Victory Arch, Saddam Husain had a copy of Faisal's statue reinstalled at the entrance to his new Haifa street. The tragic irony is that Iraq's first King, Faisal I, was Saddam Husain's polar opposite; he was the most tolerant politician in modern Iraqi history. His monument should never have been torn down in the first place, much less be reinstalled by a tyrant who was extending his legitimacy by reinstating that memory. Anyway memories leave traces behind; they cannot be completely excised.

The new generation of monuments built in the 1980s are founded upon cavernous layers of reinforced concrete buried deep under the ground; it will take more than ropes and eager hearts to bring them down this time. Maybe tearing them down isn't the answer, for other reasons. By simply gazing at the monument in the knowledge that an

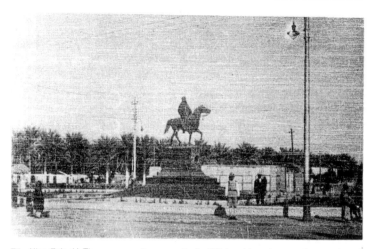

71. King Faisal I. The monument was erected in 1934 and torn down on the morning of 14 July 1958, by crowds celebrating the overthrow of the monarchy. Faisal died a broken man in 1933, aware that his policies, especially towards the patchwork of minorities that constituted Iraq, had failed. A replica of the statue was reinstalled at the entrance to Saddam Husain's new Haifa street (Figs. 13 and 14) amid much fanfare thirty-one years later on the anniversary of the revolution. Why? The point the regime wanted to make was that Ba'thism had nothing to fear from Iraqi history. The Ba'th today exude an air of timeless inevitability, a sense of connectedness with the past so profound that its terminus in their rule seems almost logical.

exact replica of His limbs was cast in bronze before their eyes, future generations might see something that words will never quite fathom. The Iraqi Ba'th have lasted longer than any other regime in the country's modern history. They are an indigenous creation, imposed by no outside power. What they did and how they ruled should not be forgotten. Like the sword of Damocles, the swords of this monument hang over Iraqis. Even if the tyrant were dead, they are obliged to confront them to exit from his spell. There are searing memories before which human beings can only stand in awe, speechless.

Suppose for a moment that the monument succeeded in outliving the inevitable reaction against it, and that Iraq were then to turn into a more ordinary kind of state, one in which it was unthinkable that such a testament to the authority of its rulers could be built. What might happen to the monument?

Nelson's column in Trafalgar Square is an ugly object which started

131

life symbolizing the victory of one set of men over another. But by now Nelson's column is part of London's memory. The city cannot do without it any more than we as individuals can banish the unpleasant memories of our childhood. What does this column signify today? War, victory, the nastiness of the French? More likely tourists, the National Gallery, home for thousands of pigeons and picture postcards which circulate the whole world over.

Cities collect objects like these, and then time transforms their meaning. Symbols of authority, somebody's victory and everyone's kitsch can turn into their opposites. This was the lesson of Pop art and Venturi's discovery of Las Vegas. Suppose some clever Iraqi Pop artist of the future, thoroughly disillusioned by war and irredeemably purged of Jewad Salim's romanticism, discovered and appropriated the monument as raw material for a new statement about art. What would he or she say about this Iraqi variant of a Campbell's soup can? Is an ironic play on Pop art the way out of the Iraqi bottleneck of *turath*-as-kitsch?

Probably not; the Arabic language does not even have a word for irony (words like *sukhriyya, hijaa', istih'zaa'*, which come closest, mean satire, sarcasm, derision or mockery). If irony is taken not as a mere swapping of 'yes' for 'no', a game of hide and seek in which the seeker knows what he is looking for, but as a genuine tension, an attraction and a repulsion, an opposition between two poles which is in the end irresolvable, then an Arabic literary tradition utilizing irony as a way of thinking about reality does not exist. Islamic culture appropriated Greek thought via Aristotle (who did not approve of irony) and in the form of Neoplatonism, which censored out the enigmatic side of Plato. Platonic irony in the sense of a journey into the unknown, even the unknowable — the humbling experience of knowing how little one knows — is itself unknown in Arabic culture; it is impossible for the traditional or classically formed Arab mind to conceive of irony even as an abstract idea.[100]

However, a modern culture (like contemporary Iraq which is unimaginable outside the twentieth century), deformed by a cult of violence and the effects of a great war, has what one might call a *need* to look at itself irreverently, uncertainly and with a little humility; it has a need to unfix its terrible fixation upon itself. This is a part of the world that experienced nationalism, socialism, communism, but never

an Enlightenment. Salman Rushdie started an important ball rolling in
The Satanic Verses. The reaction to the book proves not that he got it
wrong, but that he got something extremely fundamental dead right.
Iraqis in particular, like Muslims in general, could do with some
demystification in place of their obsession with their own history, with
turath. In the visual arts, what the painter Francis Bacon called the
'brutality of fact' might usefully take over from the genteel elegance
and classicism of, say, Henry Moore, whose vision influenced modern
Iraq's greatest artist, Jewad Salim. As against 'unity', wholeness of
existence and oneness of fate, artists, writers and intellectuals –
catering to no public, no popular masses, no state – might offer
themselves up to the winds, let themselves be partitioned up or ever so
thoroughly individualized, disaggregated and cosmopolitanized. The
struggle against the kitschness which today rots the Iraqi soul calls for
concreteness, irreverence, re-discovery of the outside, and
acknowledgement of the facticity and uncertainty of the world (itself,
incidentally, the only proof we have of our freedom). Pop may not be
much as art, but it is as outside as outside can be to the average Iraqi.
Does it have value as a tool with which to dig away at the importance
of Saddam Husain's monument? The task at hand is formidable, for
the reality is such that even irony falters and jokes stick in the throat.

The monument will one day have to be confronted, not excised.
There is no British yoke out there any longer, no king too 'soft' on
minorities, no 'Zionist' threat; Iraqis have only themselves to look to.
The responsibility for it – whether individual or collective – is a
question which invokes the entire problematic of what happened in
Iraq under the Ba'th; it is inextricably wedded to the future meaning
and destiny of the monument. Either responsibility devolves upon the
President alone, or he shares that responsibility with others. The point
is not about involving individuals (like Khalid Rahal) in the personal
actions of this President; it is about all those features of the monument
that unselfconsciously encompass both him and them.

How is it possible that such an object came to represent, for
however short a while, the city I was born and brought up in? This is a
question every thinking Iraqi ought to examine. The problem of
collective responsibility for Saddam Husain's monument can only be
one of *knowing* the thing to be vulgar and kitsch and then *feeling*
weighed down by that knowledge. What will future generations of

Iraqis see in this monument: a symbol of the demonic machinations of one man which they will once again try to tear down on the day of his overthrow, or an unforgettable testament to their country's years of shame?

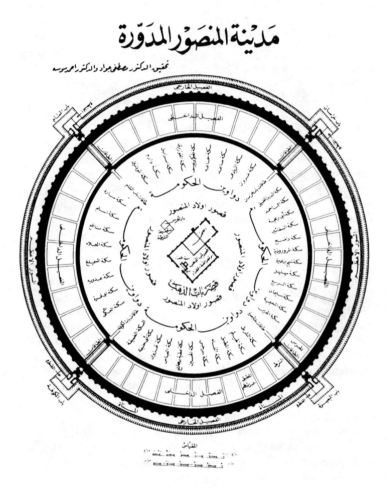

Notes

1. The Round City of Baghdad with its four gateways as built by the second Abbasid Caliph, Abu Ja'far al-Mansur, in 762 A D. Very detailed descriptions with street names have been provided by classical Arab authors on the basis of which this plan was reconstructed. The original city has disappeared entirely and the site is built over so it cannot be excavated. At the centre is the 'Palace of the Golden Door', used by al-Mansur with its 'Green Dome'. The enclosed *sahan* (grand courtyard) of the central mosque of the city juts out from the central square of the palace. Al-Mansur's sons resided in the first circular layer surrounding the centre, which is in turn followed by the *diwans* (departments) of government. The river Tigris does not enter at all as a factor in the planning; it merely passes by the Kufa gate (bottom left) as though by accident. Note the double tier of fortifications around the city and the combination of mosque and palace at the geometrical centre of the conception. Nearness to the centre, whether defined as the person of the Caliph or as the true word of God, was what counted above everything else in matters of power, spirituality, privilege and obligation. This city is truly a piece of ideology walled off from the world. The first Westerner to record a description of Baghdad was Marco Polo in 1271 A D, by which time the city walls had grown irregular and the Tigris bounded it on one side. The plan was prepared by two eminent Iraqi scholars: the historian, Dr Mustapha Jewad, and the archaelogist, Dr Ahmad Sousa.

2. Conrad Fiedler, *On Judging Works of Visual Art* (Berkeley: University of California Press, 1957), 60.

3. ibid., 44.

4. I have it from a reliable source that the idea to cast the arms came from the President himself. However, it was clearly taken at a later stage in the development of the concept because the arms are not present in the sketch publicized by the regime (see Fig. 3). A different source contends that the idea was the executing sculptor's, Khalid al-Rahal. The issue will probably never be resolved because Rahal is now dead.

5. I am borrowing the concept of 'aura' utilized by Walter Benjamin in his influential essay, 'The Work of Art in the Age of Mechanical Reproduction', published in a collection of his essays entitled *Illuminations* (New York: Schocken, 1969). The implications of the Victory Arch appearing twice, not once, at either end of a ceremonial axis which is itself part of a larger, Nuremburg-style military parade ground, is discussed at the beginning of Chapter 6 on 'Vulgarity and Art'.

6. Hannah Arendt, *The Origins of Totalitarianism* (New York: Harcourt Brace & Jovanovich, 1973), 382.

7. Amir Iskander, *Saddam Husain: Munadhilan wa Mufakiran wa Insanan* (Paris: Hachette, 1980), 18 and 21 respectively.

8. For a marvellous exposition of how the language and images of the French Revolution served a similar purpose, see Lynn Hunt, *Politics, Culture, and Class in the French Revolution* (Berkeley: University of California Press, 1984), especially Part One entitled 'The Poetics of Power'.

9. From the argument in Jon Elster, *Ulysses and the Sirens: Studies in Rationality and Irrationality* (Cambridge: Cambridge University Press, revised 1984 edition), 50.

10. The reference is to Socrates' 'noble lie' in *The Republic*, Book III, designed to provide an account of the origin of the good city and the 'natural' inequalities (of honours bestowed, degrees of virtue, shares in ruling) which exist within it.

11. Taken from a joint statement written in 1943 by these three giants of early modernism entitled 'Nine Points on Monumentality'. Republished in the *Harvard Architecture Review IV*, Spring 1984, MIT Press, 62–3.

12. As reported by the artist in an interview with him on the monument in *Gilgamesh: A Journal of Modern Iraqi Art* (Baghdad: Ministry of Information & Culture, no. 3, 1987), 15.

13. From the pamphlet entitled *Nasb Shuhadaa' Qadisiyyat Saddam*, issued by Amanat al-Assima, Baghdad, 1983, 3 and 1. Information on the monument is taken from this document which is accompanied by drawings and photographs.

14. *National Geographic*, vol. 167, no. 1, January 1985. See the article by Sharbil Daghir in *Al-Hayat*, no. 9508, 8 November 1989, p. 10.

15. From the introductory article, 'Baghdad: Breaking Tides', *Process: Architecture*, no. 58 (Tokyo: May 1985), 21–5. The whole issue is devoted to 'new' Baghdad, and is entitled 'Medinat al-Salaam [the city of Peace]: Baghdad 1979–83'.
   A similarly celebratory article entitled 'Baghdad Resurgent' by Sherban Cantacuzino, former editor of the *Architectural Review* and presently Secretary of the Royal Fine Art Commission of Britain, appeared in *Mimar 6* (Singapore: Concept Media, October–December 1982), 56–71. Also see 'Urban Renaissance in Baghdad', *Albenna*, vol. 4, no. 21–22 (Riyadh: Dar al-Finoon al-Saudiyya, April–May 1985), 76–88.

16. Along with virtually every resident Iraqi architect, the following important names in international architecture were among those who received commissions from Saddam Husain (not all of which were built due

to the war. I list only a representative sampling of the work): The Architects Collaborative (Gropius's old firm), USA, did the master plan for Khulafa street, an extension to the Khulafa mosque and the Sheraton hotel; Sheppard Robson, UK (a high-rise building on the same street); Venturi and Rauch, USA (shops and offices complex along with the Baghdad State Mosque Competition); Arthur Erikson Associates, Canada (the master plan for Abu Nuwas area); Arup Associates, UK (Bab al-Sheikh development); Ricardo Bofill, Spain (Baghdad State Mosque and Bab al-Sheikh); M and R International, Belgium (Haifa street buildings); Richard England, Malta (project in Haifa street); Jorgen Bo Associates; Carlfried Mutschler, West Germany (shopping centre and housing); John Warren and APP, UK (conservation around al-Gailani mosque); Van Treek, France; Finnconsult, Finland (Baghdad island development); Skaarup & Jesperson (Abu Nuwas housing scheme); TEST (Haifa street projects).

17. Aldo Rossi, *Selected Writings and Projects* (London: Architectural Design, 1983), 23. Rossi is an Italian architect and theorist whose writings place a particular importance upon monuments as the quintessential urban artefact, and are among the most important post-war contributions to rethinking the tenets of early modernism in relation to the city.

18. From interview with Amir Iskander, in *Saddam Husain*, op. cit., 320.

19. The phrase is from Fiedler, op. cit., p. 43, and is meant by him to refer only to the artist.

20. The statement is worth quoting in full: 'Like this average man, they experience a split between their methods of thinking and their methods of feeling. The feeling of those who govern and administer the countries is untrained and still imbued with the pseudo-ideals of the nineteenth century. This is the reason why they are not able to recognize the creative forces of our period, which alone could build the monuments or public buildings that should be integrated into new urban centers which can form a true expression of our epoch.' My point of course is precisely that Saddam Husain does not experience such a split. Whether he should or not is, of course, an entirely separate question. Taken from 'Nine Points on Monumentality', in the *Harvard Architecture Review IV*, 62–3.

21. From a 1977 speech published in a volume containing Saddam Husain's thoughts on how history should be taught in Iraq. See Saddam Husain, *Hawla Kitabat al-Tarikh* (Baghdad: Dar al-Hurriyya, 1979), 23.

22. Saddam Husain, *Al-Dimuqratiyya Masdar Quwwah lil-fard wa al-Mujtama'* (Baghdad: al-Thawra publications, 1977), 19–21.

23. Michel 'Aflaq, *Fi Sabil al-Ba'th* (Beirut: Dar al-Tali'ah, 1959), 29–30.

24. Albert Speer, *Inside the Third Reich* (New York: Weidenfeld and Nicolson, 1970), 40, 80.

25. John Ruskin was the most influential art critic of the nineteenth century. His ideas came under attack by the Modern Movement but are being revived in these post-modern days. In a curious way, Ruskin foresaw Speer's problem and provided the justification that Speer clearly needed but did not spell out: 'I think a building cannot be considered as in its prime until four or five centuries have passed over it; and that the entire choice and arrangement of its details should have reference to their appearance after that period ...' *The Seven Lamps of Architecture* (New York: The Noonday Press, 1961), 183.

26. Speer, *Inside the Third Reich*, op. cit., 56.

27. From the poem 'Auguries of Innocence' by William Blake (1757–1827).

28. From the essay 'New York Pop', in Lucy R. Lippard, *Pop Art* (London: Thames and Hudson, 1970), 86, 87.

29. ibid., 97–8.

30. From the entry on Andy Warhol by Alistair Mackintosh in *Contemporary Artists*, ed. Colin Naylor and Genesis P-Orridge (New York: St Martin's Press, 1977), 1030.

31. From the essay 'Theatrum Philosophicum' by Michel Foucault, in *Language, Counter-memory, Practice: Selected Essays and Interviews* (Ithaca: Cornell University Press, 1977). All quotes taken from between pages 186–90.

Magritte is also an interesting painter from a Foucaultian point of view. He was not interested in painterly aesthetics, or in painting as an end in itself. To him poetry was superior to painting and he liked to consider himself a thinker who happened to communicate with paint. In his essay on Magritte, *This Is Not A Pipe* (California: University of California Press, 1983), Foucault manages to tease out some of Magritte's own complexity while expanding his idea of 'non-affirmative painting'. By this Foucault means a type of painted discourse which constantly disorients through the play of words and images until finally it collapses of its own weight. The weapon of this collapse, of this destruction of what is uniquely visual about the medium, is the ascendancy of the principles of similitude and repetition over the classical ones (as Foucault sees art history) of resemblance and affirmation (plastic representation of a model outside the painting). Magritte is a crucial stepping stone along that path. But the climax of the ascent is of course Andy Warhol. Foucault ends his essay on Magritte with this tantalizing sentence: 'A day will come when, by means of similitude relayed indefinitely along the length of a series, the image itself, along with the name it bears, will lose its identity. Campbell, Campbell, Campbell, Campbell': ibid., 54.

32. Robert Venturi, Denise Scott Brown, Steven Izenour, *Learning from Las Vegas: The Forgotten Symbolism of Architectural Form* (Cambridge: The MIT Press, 1977, revised edition), 50.

33. In Iraq such arches have been used on somewhat less auspicious occasions. In the summer of 1933, the year after the country achieved formal political independence, a popular army-led pogrom of the Assyrian community went into full swing. After a gruesome massacre in the village of Sumayl on 11 August, triumphal arches were set up to celebrate in the city of Mosul. According to the account given by a British inspector based in Mosul, the arches were 'decorated with melons stained with blood and with daggers stuck into them. This delicate representation of the heads of the slain Assyrians was in keeping with the prevailing sentiment': R.S. Stafford, *The Tragedy of the Assyrians* (London: Allen & Unwin Ltd, 1935), 201. Perhaps the first antecedent for Saddam Husain's monument in modern Iraq was this hastily erected 'popular' arch of 1933.

34. Shown on 'Rear Window', Channel 4, 23 May 1990.

35. Quentin Bell, *Bad Art* (Chicago: The University of Chicago Press, 1989), 13.

36. ibid., 16.

37. Robert Venturi, *Complexity and Contradiction in Architecture* (New York: The Museum of Modern Art, 1966), 48, 50.

38. Venturi, Brown, Izenour, *Learning from Las Vegas*, op. cit., 117.

39. See ibid., 90. See also the critique of Venturi's architecture in Kenneth Frampton, *Modern Architecture: A Critical History* (London: Thames and Hudson, 1985), 291.

40. The President's words are quoted in an article devoted to the scheme in the Baghdad weekly, *Alif Baa'* (date missing), 33–6.

41. From an interview with Bofill, in Warren A. James, *Ricardo Bofill, Taller de Arquitectura: Buildings and Projects 1960–1985* (New York: Rizzoli, 1988), 186.

42. Taken from the Venturi, Rauch and Scott Brown statement of 'Design Philosophy' for the Baghdad State Mosque. Published, along with all the designs submitted, by Amanat al-Asima (1983), 56.

43. Charles Jencks, *The Language of Post-Modern Architecture*, revised edition (London: Academy, 1978), 113. I am indebted to the writings of Jencks on Post-Modernism for stimulating new ways of asking old questions.

44. The occasion was a conference on architecture and heritage chaired by the President (see next chapter). One day, to everyone's consternation, he simply didn't show up and appeared instead in army fatigues on national television to announce to the world why he had to launch a war instead of getting on with the conference.

45. A list of some of the architects involved and their projects is given in note 16.

46. *Architecture Without Architects* is the title of Bernard Rudofsky's influential book which followed a 1964 exhibition of the same title at the Museum of Modern Art (New York: Doubleday & Company, 1964). The profound influence of 'primitive art' on modern painting and sculpture was covered in a major exhibition in MoMA and treated in a two-volume study, William Rubin (ed.), *'Primitivism' in Twentieth-Century Art* (New York, 1984).

47. The phrase used by Jencks in *The Language of Post-Modern Architecture*, op. cit., 21.

48. See the article by Charles Jencks, 'The New Classicism and its Emergent Rules', in *Architectural Design*, vol. 58, no. 12, 1988.

49. From his definition of 'Kitsch' in 'Sixty-Three Words', *The Art of the Novel* (New York: Grove Press, 1988), 135.

50. Paul Valéry, *The Art of Poetry*, (Princeton: Princeton University Press, Bollingen Series XLV. 7, 1985), 56.

51. See the article by Jabra I. Jabra, '"How To Arabize My Art?" ... Art First, or the Artist?', in the Arabic daily, *Al-Hayat*, 25 September 1989.

52. For instance: in November 1988, two major Olympic-style events were held in Baghdad. The first was an international exhibition for the plastic arts with several thousand works exhibited representing six hundred artists from all over the world. Twenty-three 'prizes' were awarded (including six gold medals) and 15,000 Iraqi dinars to each 'winner'. See the 7 November report in the London Arabic daily, *Asharq al-Awsat*. On the 24 November, the ninth Mirbid Arabic poetry festival was held under the title 'The Mirbid of Victory'. The most famous names in poetry, literature and criticism from nineteen Arab countries attended (including Nazar Qabani, Mahmood Darwish, 'Abd al-Wahab Bayati, Ghada al-Saman). Prizes in the form of a Saddam Husain medal for the arts were duly awarded to the 'winners'.

53. The full transcript of the speech appeared in the official Baghdad daily, *Al-'Iraq*, 16 September 1980.

54. From the witty article by Paul Routledge, 'Left Speechless by the New Babel', *Observer*, 6 November 1988.

55. Quoted in a report on the project by Paul Lewis in the *New York Times*, 19 April 1989. See also his extended report in the Sunday travel section of the *New York Times*, 25 June 1989, 8–9.

56. Eric Hobsbawm and Terence Ranger (eds), *The Invention of Tradition* (Cambridge: Cambridge University Press, 1987), 4. In the introduction

Hobsbawm defines his terms. The book then deals with seven case studies: rituals of the British monarchy (1820–1977), creating a Scottish Highland tradition, Welsh romanticism, mass-producing traditions in Europe (1870–1914), Colonial Africa, and representing authority in Victorian India.

57. *Process: Architecture*, no. 58, 102. See section on 'Conservation Projects'.

58. In an interview, the artist Ismail Fattah had this to say about the origins of the Martyrs' Monument: 'I insisted on having an open space ... Big monuments are originally from the East ... the Pyramids, the Obelisk, the Spiral Minarets, etc. ... The earth is flat, so these monuments can be seen from all directions ... In the beginning I had several attempts such as an idea of having the martyr bursting from the centre. But I did not like it – it was too theatrical. Then, the idea of life versus death began to form. The two pieces moving together towards martyrdom and fertility and the life stream. I moved the pieces until I got the interplay I wanted.' Taken from *Gilgamesh: A Journal of Modern Iraqi Art* (Baghdad: Dar al-Ma'mun, 1987), no. 3, 15–16.

59. See for instance the appreciation by Jabra I. Jabra, 'From Miniature to Monument: The Creative Quest of Mohammed Ghani', in *UR*, May–July 1979, 26–35, published in London.

60. From the interview with Ghani in the Arabic daily, *Asharq al-Awsat*, 12 September 1988. See also his comments to William Ellis published in 'The New Face of Baghdad', *National Geographic*, vol. 167, no. 1, January 1985, 107.

61. Jewad Salim's opening statement at the first exhibition held in 1951 for the 'Baghdad Group for Modern Art' which he founded. Reprinted in full in Jabra I. Jabra's book, *Jewad Salim wa Nasb al-Hurriyya* (Baghdad: Ministry of Information, 1974), 191–3.

62. From the account given by Shakir Hasan aal Said in chapter 10, 'The Emergence of a Civilizational Personality – The Baghdad Group for Modern Art', of the two-volume study *Fusool min Tarikh al-Haraka al-Tashkilliyah fi al-Iraq* (Baghdad: Ministry of Education and Information, 1983), 172. Said's history of the visual arts 'movement' in Iraq is important because it combines insights from a very talented artist who lived through the period, with a strikingly ideological-political interpretation of that history, repeatedly emphasizing the 'collective' (spirit, vision, purpose) over the individual as though that had to be the virtue of art.

63. From the foreword to the exhibition catalogue, *Lebanon – The Artist's View: 200 Years of Lebanese Painting* (London: Quartet Books, 1989) written by Sir Hugh Casson, former President of the Royal Academy of Arts. The excellent article by John Carswell in the book entitled 'The Lebanese Vision', discusses the specificity of the Lebanese experience.

64. Hasan, *Fusool*, op. cit. (note 62), 163.

65. 'Continuity' with the past first appeared as a central theme in the written statement of principles put out by the 'Baghdad Group for Modern Art' in 1951. But then it was still contentious and new; today it is a cliché. See extracts in Hasan, ibid., 166.

66. ibid., 164, 176, and chapter 10 generally.

67. See Hasan, *Fusool*, vol. 1, 108, 124−5.

68. For the passage from Satia' al-Husri to Sami Shawkat in the political culture of Iraqi pan-Arabism, see Samir al-Khalil, *Republic of Fear* (Berkeley: University of California Press, 1989), chapter 5.

69. See the 1974 Political Report of the Eighth Congress of the Arab Ba'th Socialist Party, published under the title *The 1968 Revolution in Iraq* (London: Ithaca Press, 1979).

70. The interpretation of the riderless horse is based on Jabra's conversations with the artist. See *Jewad Salim wa Nasb al-Hurriyya*, op. cit. (note 61), 136.

71. See ibid., 152, 148.

72. In a pamphlet entitled *The Monument in Memory of the Glorious Revolution of July 14th* (Baghdad, 1961: no page numbers), by Fadhel Mohammed al-Bayati, issued on the occasion of its unveiling, the centre section is interpreted as follows:

> It is the immortal July 14th.
> The proud soldier's great and dazzling leap, embodying the strength of the saviour and revolutionary Leader who rebelled for the sake of the people, his muscles tense, his fist shattering prison bars in all directions. His body has burst out of the people like an explosion, and the gun-holding hand is reinforced with the people's hand.
> It is the dawn of the Revolution which put an end to the annals of tragedy and translated the force of Iraq's people into constructive energy. The disc above is the sun, light after darkness. It is one of Iraq's oldest symbols. Here [in ancient Mesopotamia] the sun first rose to illumine the world, and here the Revolution's sun first rose, led by its fearless soldier ['Abdul Karim Qassem]. With his foot the soldier has trampled upon a shield representing evil. It is the shield behind which took shelter all reigns of tyranny and corruption.

73. For a general survey, see 'Modern Arab Art' by the Palestinian artist Kamal Boullata in *Finoon Arabiah*, no. 6, vol. 2, 1982, 29−40. Note Boullata's appreciation of the place of Jewad Salim in the development of Arab figurative art, 37.

74. Dr Shams al-Din Faris, *Al-Manabia'al-Tarikhiyya lil-fan al-Jidari fi al-*

'*Iraq al-Mua'assir* (Baghdad: Ministry of Information, Art Series, no. 24, 1974), 60–63 and Introduction.

75. Hasan, *Fusool*, op. cit., vol. 1, 211.

76. The phrase is Jabra's in *Jewad Salim wa Nasb a-Hurriyya*, op. cit., 72. Al-Bayati's pamphlet dedicated to 'Abd al-Karim Qassem, the Leader of the 14 July 1958 revolution, opens like this:

> When for the first time in 2,600 years of Iraq's long history an Iraqi artist was asked to express in sculpture, and with absolute freedom, his noble vision, he cast in bronze an epic representing the Revolution of July 14th, with its deep roots in the nation's history, its sweeping power, and its confident progress towards the freedom and prosperity of Iraq. For this large monument, made by Jewad Salim, portrays the Revolution with all its lofty ideals, a magnificent expression of the people's revolution and aspirations, realising, at the same time, a fulfilment of the artist's concept of an Iraqi style derived from the soil and tradition of this great country.

77. The book is Jabra I. Jabra's, *Judhoor al-Fan al-'Iraqi* (Baghdad: al-Dar al-'Arabiyya, 1986). The intellectual decline that such a book represents can be appreciated by comparing it with the quality and vigour of Jabra's earlier writings on art. I am thinking of the marvellous collection of early 1960s essays entitled *Al-Rihla al-Thamina* (Beirut: al-Dar al-'Arabiyya, reprinted 1979).

78. W.H. Auden, 'The Poet and the City', in *The Dyer's Hand and Other Essays* (New York: Vintage Books, 1968 edition), 85.

79. See Richard Rorty's powerful critique of essentialist theories of language, selfhood and community in *Contingency, Irony and Solidarity* (Cambridge: Cambridge University Press, 1989). Or Alasdair MacIntyre's account of the 'interminable character' of moral thinking today. By this he means not only that they go on and on, 'but also they apparently can find no terminus'. See *After Virtue* (Notre Dame: University of Notre Dame Press, 1984, second edition), 6. The problem is neatly summed up in the title of a recent collection of essays, *Universal Abandon? The Politics of Postmodernism*, ed. Andrew Ross (Minneapolis: University of Minnesota Press, 1988).

80. Hannah Arendt, *Eichmann in Jerusalem: A Report on the Banality of Evil* (London: Penguin, 1984; first published 1963).

81. See the discussion of this in Elisabeth Young-Bruehl's biography *Hannah Arendt: For Love of the World* (New Haven: Yale University Press, 1982), chapter 8, 'Cura Posterior: Eichmann in Jerusalem', 328–79.

82. Saddam Husain's Iraq is not Idi Amin's Uganda. Like Hitler's Germany,

it rests on an authority that has been legitimated. That is a theme explored in al-Khalil, *Republic of Fear* op. cit., (note 68).

83. See Jean-Jacques Rousseau, *Politics and the Arts* (Ithaca, New York: Cornell University Press, 1977), 34–47.

84. 'If a poet meets an illiterate peasant, they may not be able to say much to each other, but if they both meet a public official, they share the same feeling of suspicion; neither will trust one further than he can throw a grand piano . . .' Auden, *The Dyer's Hand*, 88–9.

85. See ibid., 78–80.

86. The classic cases are those of Thoreau and Emerson. But as Morton and Lucia White have shown in their book *The Intellectual Versus the City* (Oxford: Oxford University Press, 1977 edition), the tradition of romantic anti-urbanism includes Hawthorne, Poe, Melville, James Fenimore Cooper, Frank Norris, Frank Lloyd Wright and Lewis Mumford, among many others.

87. Chapter 6, 'The Formation of the Ba'th', in al-Khalil, *Republic of Fear*, op. cit., analyses 'Aflaq's political romanticism.

88. Rousseau, *Politics and the Arts*, op. cit., 23.

89. Quoted from the 1951 Princeton lectures of Jacques Maritain, published as *The Responsibility of the Artist* (New York: Scribner, 1960), 86.

90. ibid., 105.

91. ibid., 94.

92. A point very nicely made by Maritain in ibid., 99–101.

93. *The Oxford English Dictionary*, vol. 12 (Oxford: Clarendon Press, 1978 edition), 326.

94. I am indebted to the PhD thesis by Ifeanyi Anthony Menkiti entitled *Collective Responsibility* (Harvard University, Department of Philosophy, 1974) for some of the general points made here.

95. Paul Valéry, *The Art of Poetry*, op. cit., 236.

96. See the article by Joel Feinberg, 'Collective Responsibility', in the *Journal of Philosophy*, vol. LXV, no. 21, 7 November 1968, 680.

97. The mass murder of Iraqi Kurds was widely reported in the Western press following the chemical attack on the town of Halabja in 1987 in which 5,000 people died. However, the gassing of army deserters in the Shi'a regions of the south is less widely known. See the report by Helga Graham in the *Guardian*, 15 September 1988.

98. In *Republic of Fear*, I estimated a total of 677,000 institutionally armed

men in 1980 (i.e. just before the decision taken in the spring of 1980 to launch the Iraq—Iran war). This represents one-fifth of the econonomically active labour force, a number that is by any standard completely out of proportion with the size of the country. A historical account of the legitimation of the Ba'th in Iraq is provided in the second half of the book.

99. From an article by Hannah Arendt first published in 1945 on the dilemma of Nazi war crimes whose argument I have been broadly following: 'Organized Guilt and Universal Responsibility', reprinted in Roger W. Smith (ed.), *Guilt: Man and Society* (New York: Anchor Books, 1971), 261.

100. On the central place of irony in Plato, see Paul Friedlander, *Plato: An Introduction* (Princeton: Princeton University Press, Bollingen Series LIX, 1969).

Index
Figures in italics refer to captions